Liberty Lost?

Three Great Evils...
And the Coming Great Awakening

HAROLD MICHAEL PHILLIPS, TH.D.

Liberty Lost?
Three Great Evils …
And the Coming Great Awakening?

Copyright ©2021

ACKNOWLEDGEMENTS

I would like to say a deep thanks to my family for their continued patience for the time I was involved in studying and writing this book. There were many days that I was found in deep study when I was needed by them. I appreciate their love and understanding. I especially thank my wife for her encouragement over the years. Thank you, Corkie, my best friend.

I thank Pleasant View Baptist Church, in Port Deposit, Maryland, for the inspiration to continue in labor for Christ. I thank all the members for their inspiration and encouragement. I would also say a hardy thanks to Bear Spring Baptist Church of Dover, Tennessee, Sylvia Baptist Church of Dickson, Tennessee, Eunity Baptist Church of Cheraw, South Carolina, Trace Creek Baptist Church of Mayfield, Kentucky, Flat Rock Baptist Church of Starr, South Carolina, and Friendship Baptist Church of Honea Path, South Carolina for their love, patience and investment in my Christian growth.

I also would like to thank my parents Billy Ray and Annie Ruth Phillips, my brothers Brian, Steve and David Phillips, and my sister, Cathy Kennedy, for their encouragement these past years. Thanks so much for being there.

I also give a word of thanks to those who have labored before me to bring this evidence to light. Others have laid the foundation upon which I am building. Thank you.

Thanks also to Bart Thomas and Gayle Leubecker for their labor as we brought this book together. Thanks.

TABLE OF CONTENTS

INTRODUCTION

This book is dedicated to sounding an alarm to all mankind interested in God, God's Word, America and its future, or even the future of the world. We are experiencing the fruits of two great tragedies in this country. We are right now allowing a third tragedy to take place without much opposition at all.

These three tragedies are:

1. *The erosion of Creation by Evolution;*
2. *The erasing of Christian History in America;*
3. *The "watering down" of the Precious Word of God.*

It's a simple case of cause and effect—but it's also a case of God either blessing or withdrawing His blessing.

I want to point out to the reader of this book the fruits that followed the crumbling of the foundations of Creation and Christian History. But the crumbling of the Word of God is the foundation we will not be able to endure. This will be the Tidal Wave to Come. This will be a wave that will wipe out all truth. We, at this time, can still say, "Thus Saith the Lord," but it is short lived.

I intend to inform you about the extreme damage being done every day by new translations and modern books proclaiming to be, and being accepted as, Bibles or the total word of God.

America has been called the big experiment by some. For over 200 years the United States of America has been "The Shining Light on the Hill," as well as an example of what God can do when we believe in Him and claim Jesus as our King.

Even the phrase, "We have no King but Jesus," was the war cry as the colonies were fighting for their freedom from England during the Revolutionary war.

A History Declaration:

In the year 1752, in the month of August, The Liberty Bell was cast in England by order of the Pennsylvania assembly to commemorate the fiftieth anniversary of the colony's existence. The inscription on the bell comes straight out of the twenty-fifth chapter of the third book of the Bible, Leviticus. The inscription cast onto the bell reads, "Proclaim liberty through all the land and to all the inhabitants thereof." The Liberty Bell got its name for being rung July 8, 1776 at the first reading of the Declaration of Independence.

George Washington, the man referred to as the father of America, is a wonderful example of these beliefs. Washington's prayer for the United States of America appears on a plaque in St. Paul's Chapel in New York, as well as at Pohick Church, Fairfax County, Virginia, where Washington was a vestryman from 1763 to 1784:

"Almighty God; We make our earnest prayer that Thou wilt keep the United States in Thy holy protection; and Thou wilt incline the hearts of the citizens to cultivate a spirit of subordination and obedience to government; and entertain a brotherly affection and love for one another and for their fellow citizens of the United States at large, and particularly for their brethren who have served in the field.

And finally that Thou wilt most graciously be pleased to dispose us all to do justice, to love mercy, and to demean ourselves with that charity, humility, and pacific temper of mind which were the characteristics of the Divine Author of our blessed religion, and without a humble imitation of whose example in these things we can never hope to be a happy nation.

Grant our supplication, we beseech Thee, through Jesus Christ our Lord. Amen."

Even up to 1954, the Congress of the United States, on June 14, 1954, voted to add the words, "under God" to the Pledge of Allegiance.

The points of unity and power were all empowered by statements like, "In God We Trust," or "Endowed by their Creator…" Our unfailing trust and unapologetic statements of our dependence on God were clear and factual.

Note these scriptures of interest:

Psalms 11:3 *"If the foundations be destroyed, what can the righteous do?"*

John 14:1 *"Let not your heart be troubled: ye believe in God, believe also in me."*

2nd Corinthian 3:17 *"… and where the Spirit of the Lord is, there is Liberty."*

These verses and a thousand other ones remind us that our Peace and our Liberties are all gifts that come as a part of our being a country built upon God's Word. Statements such as God's trusted Word and that this trusted Word declares that we believe in a creator and we trust in His Son for our help.

A thought before we get into the meat of this information:

What does Liberty look like?

Jesus said, as He started His ministry, that He had come to bring liberty, and that He would set the captives free (recorded in the book of Luke chapter 2). Paul wrote to the Church in Galatia and he said that liberty was available so we could love people in a pure way (Galatians 5: 13).

But in your mind, what does liberty/freedom really look like?

1. Sleeping in your home without even locking the doors?
2. Sending your children to play in the city park and not having to worry about them?
3. Walking down the street in a major city in America without fear of being robbed or killed?
4. Going to Washington, D.C. and visiting the Capital Building or the White House without fences?

These are images of freedoms that existed in America not too many years ago; but think about these issues we experience in America today.

I am calling this book *Liberty Lost?* for a specific reason. There was a book written during the mid-1600s by John Milton called *Paradise Lost*. This was an epic poem that tells of the war for Heaven as man was put out of Eden and Satan was put out of Heaven. This book *Liberty Lost?* discusses the wonderful freedoms we have experienced for over 200 years that are disappearing quickly because we are allowing these three foundations to dissolve.

Let's talk about this…

CHAPTER ONE

THE FIRST WAVE
ERODING THE CREATION FOUNDATION

If the foundations be destroyed,
what can the righteous do?
-- PSALM 11:3

I. EVOLUTION: FACT OR FAITH?

According to Noah Webster:

Science-- *Art derived from precepts or built on principles. Science is knowledge, or certain comprehension or understanding of truth or facts by the mind. Science is a collection of the general principles or leading truths relating to any subject. Science is knowledge gained by studying present material using the five senses.*

Religion-- *This word seems originally to have signified an oath or vow to the gods, or the obligation of such oath or vow which was held very sacred. Religion is the faith or worship of a supreme being. Religion is faith in something that will influence all aspects of life, to the degree that a person believes.*

Science is supposed to be a total collection of knowledge gathered by using the five senses to study present material. Science is not man's opinion. The fact is that anything other than the evidence presented is not science, but a belief pushed without science to prove or support a belief.

Wait just a minute! I thought you said religion was a belief driven by faith, and science is a study based on evidence studied. That is correct. Well, then, if that's true, if evolution is a science, it will be a study of evidence. Let's study the scientific evidence.

Now I know what you are thinking: "Certainly those who teach and accept evolution must base their system of beliefs on some evidence." (Notice I said system of beliefs.) It is true they use a few examples they call evolution. These will be discussed later in this study.

A scientist or teacher is influenced by the last 100 years of Darwin's teaching. The sinful world was looking for an answer for the question of its beginning other than God. They were looking for some way to reject God and still be respected and able to respect themselves. Therefore, when Darwin's teaching came along, the world that didn't want to answer to God jumped at the chance to say they didn't believe in God. Now they could be self-respected atheists. They had an answer that, to them, made a lot of sense. However, science had little or no evidence that Darwin's theory was credible. Even Darwin knew it was a theory that had lots of problems.

But the atheistic world was so happy to have a story to tell itself to get out from under the "God teaching," that it jumped at the chance and made Darwin its hero.

I want you to know that the science of evolution being taught today in our schools is not science and evidence at all, but the religion of Humanism. They have no scientific evidence to prove evolution. It is a theory and that is all. The scientists have fooled society into thinking that they are teaching science, when in truth they are teaching humanistic theories of beliefs that the scientists' groups have agreed must have happened. This is a series of beliefs and not science at all. Therefore, they are teaching religion—the religion of Humanism. Remember what religion is? A system of beliefs based on faith. The scientific community is teaching a system of beliefs based on faith. They, in turn, tell Christians that they cannot teach their beliefs in the schools, but the evolutionist is teaching his system of beliefs every day. They teach evolution as a science without evidence, when, in reality, they are teaching what they believe without evidence. This makes it a religion, not science at all.

You are saying, "Come on! There's got to be some evidence. Doesn't scientific evidence support evolution?" The simple answer is no. The scientific community even knows they do not have the evidence to support their beliefs. They have even put together a group of excuses for the lack of evidence. They do not deny the evidence is missing; they simply explain it in one of three ways:

1. *Some say evolution is so slow you cannot see the evidence; therefore, it cannot be proved.*
2. *Some say evolution is so fast we missed it; therefore, it cannot be proved.*
3. *Some say evolution has already stopped; therefore, it cannot be proved.*

It's too slow, it's too fast, or it has already stopped; therefore, it cannot be proved. If it cannot be proved, it is not a science. It becomes a belief, and it becomes a religion.

The question is not whether or not we teach beliefs in the public schools. The question is, whose system of beliefs can be taught? The fact is, we are in a religious war over whether or not the belief of creation or evolution is to be taught. The truth is that evolution is just masquerading as science; thus, our children are being taught a humanistic belief system that is destroying our society.

They have convinced the world that religion doesn't need to be taught in the school system to our children. But they say evolution is a science and not a belief. What do you say?

Take the story of Noah's flood for example. What do you think you would find all over the world if Noah's flood is fact? If Noah's flood is fact, you would find millions of shells and bones and pieces of animals, etc., hidden in layers of rock. What has been found? Millions of bones, and pieces of animals, etc., hidden in layers of rock. The story of the flood is just one example of the truths in the Bible substantiated by evidence found. The evidence and the story answer a lot of questions in the fossil record. But the scientific community will not even consider the biblical account of the flood. The government school system refuses to allow our children to hear about it from their teachers. Why? What are they afraid of? Maybe the children will be converted to Christianity and become sacrificial people, loving others above self, or honest people that love the truth and hate lies.

The fact is the scientific community is biased about their beliefs. But let's be honest about it; so are we Christians. We do not claim to be unbiased. All are biased in their beliefs. The only question is, from which bias does one start?

Whatever a person's bias or belief, in truth, the evidence substantiates the Bible. The study of the Bible evidence is the real science, simply because science is a study of evidence, and the Bible points out what is there – in nature, in the crust of the earth, etc., – and that is what is there. So, if true science was taught without the bias of our day, the Bible would be our most prominent science book. Does this surprise you?

I would like to point out something here. We Christians know about the theory of evolution. We are not in the dark. We have been forced to learn about it whether we wanted to or not. But that is not so about the evolution community.

They do not now about the creation foundation. Most of the unbelieving community does not know what they have been shielded from. Therefore, they really are not informed. That's sad.

The truth is, our children have been indoctrinated into a humanistic way of belief. That is, all the focus is on the human being and his needs, with no consideration of God, the afterlife or judgment day. Therefore, they live for today and become very "this world focused." "Eat, drink and be merry, for tomorrow we die." They have also been shielded from learning about the greatest giver, man of compassion and savior ever: the person of Jesus Christ. The children have been shielded from the examples of the victory of David killing the giant, Daniel in the lion's den, or Noah's ark. They have been shielded from the story of Adam and Eve. Therefore, they have lost the basic foundations for true meaning in life. They do not know why they are motivated to do wrong and cannot stop themselves at times.

We know the reason as sin nature, brought on by the sickness caused by the fruit of Adam and Eve. But they cannot make that connection, simply because they do not know the story. Of course, without the knowledge of Adam and Eve's sin curse, the story of Jesus' sacrifice has little or no meaning to them. The Great Commission is a total frustration to them as well. This is why we are experiencing such frustration from our teens of the 60s, 70s, 80s, and now 90s. Life, sin, right and wrong mean nothing to them, because of the missing pieces of knowledge. It's like you and me trying to put together a puzzle that will give us the secrets and meaning of life without all the pieces. This is so sad, and it's the beginning of sadness, not the end. We are now introducing a new group of children into society with no Bible knowledge at all. For the past 50 years we have been running on the influence of the religious teachings of our grandparents. They instilled a knowledge of and a respect for God; even the rejecters of God respected Him. But the next group will be different. You just hang on and watch, and you will see that I have shared the truth, as much as I wish it wasn't so.

The teaching of evolution is a direct teaching from the humanists, who have planned an assault on the God of the Bible. The *Humanist Manifesto* (the Humanist's statement of purpose) says plainly that it is a religion to replace all religions. There is no doubt that Humanism is a religion of the worship of man. Evolution is a part of the humanist agenda and indoctrination; therefore, Humanism and evolution go together. You really cannot have one without the other. Therefore, when evolution is taught in our schools, the religion of Humanism is being taught.

We have been fooled. They have taken the Bible out because they say we cannot teach a certain system of religious beliefs. But they replaced the biblical beliefs of Christians with the beliefs of Humanism (the worship of man). The fact is, when you take away God, the Bible and the person of Jesus from a people, you have just removed their purpose, conscience, Judge, etc. Therefore, removing the Bible from our future generations is like removing the sun from the field to be harvested. You can expect nothing but death.

I hope you will read and examine the *Humanist Manifesto* and you will verify this statement. Also, you will see that John Dewey, the father of the educational system we have today, is a signer of the *Humanist Manifesto.*

If evolution is taught so often and so dogmatically, what is the basis for their teaching, and what is their evidence of evolution? Let's take a look at a few commonly used examples...

II. FALSE FINDINGS OF EVOLUTION

The Peppered Moth

The peppered moth is used over and over again in an attempt to prove evolution. What is the peppered moth story?

The peppered moth is a case where the insect changed colors over the course of a hundred years. The peppered moth originally was mostly white, and it then gradually "adapted" to its changing environment as the pollution of the industrial revolution changed the surfaces on which the moth frequented from white to black. The darker colored moth, of course, blended in with its surroundings much better, making it more difficult for predators to spot it. Evolutionists present this example as a case for evolution.

You mean that is what the evolutionist has to prove his evolution theory? Yes, I mean that.

The evolutionist is not giving any evidence of evolution; he is simply observing the "built-in" adaptation of original God-created creatures. This is not evolving or moving from one species to another.

Fruit Fly Mutation

Darwin wrote a book called *The Origin of Species*, which could and probably should have been titled *The Fixity of Species*, because neither Darwin nor others like him have really pointed to the origin of species at all. They continue to point to micro-evolution (small changes or genetically designed variations within species) or mutations (nearly always harmful to survival and not capable of being inherited).

Mutation is, however, the result of nature after exposure to the cosmic rays that exist. A good example of that is the concern in the 1990s about the ozone layer and the rise in skin cancers. Mutation is the change in species as a result of exposure.

Scientists have taken fruit flies into the laboratory and exposed them to many different forms of radiation, and the flies do change. They change to creatures with many different variations, with strangely colored eyes and different wings. It is true that cosmic or radioactive waves do alter species, but two very important facts have been overlooked:

1. *The flies end up in a degraded state, rather than in an evolving upward state. So cosmic rays take species downward*

rather than upward. Cosmic rays destroy us; they don't improve us.

2. *We do not see cosmic rays creating species. We only see cosmic rays alter existing species. Flies are still flies when the radiation is increased or decreased.*

Also, the evolutionist says that birds extrapolate (change by breeding or climate for survival) depending on the climate. As certain birds breed with a different colored or shaped bird, they change the color or shape. But never do birds become something other than birds. Also, birds are made with specific instincts that only attract them to certain birds and not to other animals outside their species.

But some animals cannot be explained by mutation or extrapolation. They had to be created by God the way they are. Mutation does happen, but it is limited and it doesn't create or help; it hinders. Extrapolation is limited by nature itself.

Explaining the Giraffe

The evolutionist tries to explain a giraffe in a fashion that is interesting. They say that because of lack of food, the giraffe had to reach higher up for food and, therefore, extended its neck over the process of time. But the giraffe and the rest of his body don't agree. The giraffe has a terrible time drinking water, and his blood pressure is also a problem. God has designed the giraffe with a special heart pump system that sustains his strange shape. It is foolish when examining the giraffe to think that his neck grew over time when looking at other's needs. This is their idea of extrapolation.

The Woodpecker

The woodpecker is another example of the specially created creatures, and how an evolutionist explains extrapolation. The woodpecker could never have evolved into the system of survival he has. He pecks on trees and drills holes to stick his very long tongue into the hole and get out bugs. The woodpecker's beak had to be hard from the start, and his tongue had to be long from the start, or he would not have survived.

Human Development

They also once said a baby in the womb of his mother in the early stages of foundation had gills, an attached egg and a tail. When later examined, they realized that their eyes had deceived them. The gill-like items were the developing tonsils and adenoids. The egg-like object was the blood producer and the bone producer. The blood is produced in the egg-like object and actually forms the bones that exist in the baby. The "egg" is creating the bones of the child. When the bones are developed, the egg-like object disappears. The tail-like item is the end of the spine that causes the rest of the spine to develop. The spine develops, as well as the muscles attached to it. Then, when the spine develops, the tail-like object disappears.

These are examples of the scientist changing his or her mind. But the student with the wrong information most of the time never hears the correction.

Mutation is also evidenced in birth defects. We are suffering from sin, and the farther we go down in generations, we will get in worse shape. About 1% of all babies today will need medical attention of some kind when born. It is true that we have increased in medical knowledge, and we feel we are getting better. It is true that we are better informed, but we are not better physically; we have just learned more about how our body works, and now we work better with what we know. But, the truth is, we are not going up, but down.

Fixity of Species

The fact is, the evolutionist is pushing mutation as evolution when, in truth, mutation is not evolution at all. Extrapolation is also impossible. There is no way we can explain strange animal forms by either mutation or extrapolation.

Evolution is also teaching origin when, really, science is only seeing and unfolding that which already exists. Mutation and a pool of genetics bring changes of existing life, but no change beyond specific species.

The theory of evolution has dominated our society for about a century, especially in our educational institutions. The media has been most influential in promoting the "fact" of organic evolution with some television programs and magazine editorial sections loyally devoted to evolutionary viewpoint. Usually, this indoctrination is obvious and insistent, but when it is more subtle, it is nevertheless unmistakably effective.

The sadness of the whole situation is that evolution is called a science based on evidence when there is no evidence. They teach dogmatically that we are evolved from other species when, in truth, there are no fossils or evidence of this. There is no species at present in transition, etc. Think for yourselves. The biblical statement "after its kind" not only is verified by the paleontological record, but also is confirmed by modern scientific observation and experimentation.

It is possible to breed two animals in the same species and get another type of that species:

- horse and donkey = sterile mule
- zebra and horse = sterile zebronkey
- lion and tiger = sterile liger

The fact is that each of these hybrids is invariably sterile and does not reproduce. This lends strong evidence against evolution. Charles Darwin, in his writings, said himself, "Not one change of species into another is on record...we cannot prove that a single species has been changed."[i]

The Fossil Record

We now come to perhaps the most serious of defects in the evolutionary theory – the complete absence of transitional forms. If life has always been in a continual stream of transmutation from one form to another, as evolutionists insist, then we would certainly expect to find as many fossils of the intermediate stages between different forms as of the distinct kinds themselves. Yet, no fossils have been found that can be considered transitional between the major groups or phyla! From the very beginning, these organisms were just as clearly and distinctly set apart from each other as they are today. Instead of finding a record, we invariably find large gaps. This fact is absolutely fatal to the general theory of organic evolution. Even the great champion himself, Charles Darwin, acknowledged this flaw: "As by this theory, innumerable transitional forms must have existed. Why do we not find them imbedded in the crust of the earth? Why is all nature not in confusion instead of being as we see them, well-defined species? Geological research does not yield the infinitely many fine graduations between past and present species required by the theory: and this is the most obvious of the many objections which may be required against it. The explanation lies, however, in the extreme imperfection of the geological record."[ii]

While Darwin was honest enough to admit the lack of the reality and resources of the missing links, he nevertheless felt or hoped that this was only due to the incomplete fossil record. In time, he argued, these connecting links would be found and the critical gaps filled. This convenient excuse, however, no longer offers any refuge for evolution. As George Neville remarks, "There is no need to apologize any longer for the poverty of the fossil record. In some ways it has become almost unmanageably rich, and discovery is outpacing integration... The fossil record nevertheless continues to be composed mostly of gaps." [iii]

The amazing thing is that the whole concept of organic evolution is completely absurd and impossible. It is absolutely astonishing that an idea which is so devoid of any legitimate scientific evidence could have attained a position of such prestige in the name of science. However, the most widespread influential argument against the veracity of the Bible is the all-too-common belief that modern science has proven evolution, thereby discrediting the scriptural account of creation.

The fatal flaw in this argument is that it is impossible to prove any theory of origins. This is because the very essence of the scientific method is based on observation and experimentation, and it is impossible to make observations or conduct experiments on the origin of the universe. This point is conceded by British biologist L. Harrison Matthew in the forward to the 1971 edition of *Darwin's Origin of Species*: "The fact of evolution is the backbone of biology, and biology is thus in the peculiar position of being a science founded on a parallel to a belief in special creation – both are concepts which believers know to be true but neither, up to the present, has been capable of proof." [iv]

Science may speculate about the past or future, but it can only actually observe the present. Obviously, then, the widespread assumption that evolution is an established fact of science is absolutely false. Thus, evolution can only be labeled as a belief, a subjective philosophy of origins, the religion of many scientists. Despite this fact, most of today's scientists and teachers still insist that evolution is an established fact of science.

The Geologic Column

Before the nineteenth century, the vast majority of scientists interpreted earth history in terms of biblical creationism and catastrophes (Genesis flood), and consequently believed in a relatively short time scale. However, the more recent acceptance of a principle known as uniformitarianism has successfully promoted the idea of an ancient earth. Uniformitarianism is the belief that the origin and development of all things can be explained exclusively in terms of the same natural laws and processes operating today.

They believe that anything could have developed by itself given enough time. They boldly say that this world is millions of years old. They continually try to date rocks and fossils as millions of years old. But the truth is that these scientists are just talking with no evidence to prove any such thing. The oldest or earliest authenticated written record dates back to about 3,500 B.C. Prior to the existence of eyewitnesses, no one can be absolutely certain of what actually happened before that. The fact is, science finds many fossils of species that are, as far as we know today, extinct. But no fossils can be found to link one species to another. The scientific community continues to make assumptions with no evidence to prove its assumptions. The fact is that the primary evidence for evolution is the assumption of evolution.

It is important to realize that nowhere in the world does the geologic column (the geologists' timetable) actually occur. It exists only in the minds of evolutionary geologists. It is simply an idea, an ideal series of geologic systems, and not an actual column of rocks that can be observed at a particular locality. Real rock formations are characterized by gaps and reversals of this ideal, imaginary sequence. Even the Grand Canyon includes less than half of the geologic systems. In order to see the entire geologic column as it occurs in its "proper" sequential order, on would have to travel all over the world.

The fact is, the fossils that should be found at the bottom of the Grand Canyon are found in layers at the top of the Grand Canyon layered in rock. You never hear about this fact, but it is very true. The biggest hindrance to the theory of evolution is the evidence that should be its greatest support, the geological study.

Did Dinosaurs & Men Walk Together?

There are a number of known scientific facts which raise serious questions concerning the geologic column and timetable. One example would be the existence of numerous contemporaneous human and dinosaur prints found in Mexico, New Mexico, Arizona, Missouri, Kentucky, Illinois, and in other U.S. localities. These tracks are widely distributed, and are usually only exposed by flood erosion or bulldozers. They have actually been studied and verified by reliable paleontologists, and cannot be dismissed as frauds. Furthermore, there are places in Arizona and Rhodesia where dinosaur pictographs drawn by man have been found on cave or canyon walls. The obvious implication is that man once lived contemporaneously with the dinosaurs, contrary to the commonly accepted chronology of the geologic column and timetable. An Old Testament book in the Bible, Job, contains interesting references in Job 40:15 and 41:34 which seem to refer to land and marine dinosaurs living in Job's day.

Five-toed llamas allegedly became extinct about 30 million years ago, according to the evolutionary framework. Yet, archeologists have found pottery with etchings of five-toed llamas on it. Skeletons of five-toed llamas have also been found in association with the Tiahuanacan culture.

An ancient Mayan relief sculpture of a bird resembling the archaeopteryx has been found. This indicates a discrepancy of about 130 million years. If the geologic column is correct, the two should never have met. Apparently, the geological column is in error.

An amazing discovery was made by William Meister on June 1, 1968 in Utah. He found the fossil of several trilobites in the fossilized sandaled footprint of a man! But, according to the evolutionary timetable worked out in the geologic column, trilobites became extinct 230 million years before the appearance of man! Thus, to find a modern, sandal-shod man existing contemporaneously with trilobites is utter devastating to the geologic column and evolutionary framework.

Other Areas to Explore

There are other areas that would be of interest to you, if you would like to research further:

1. Radioactive dating
2. Earth's magnetic field
3. Meteoritic dust
4. The Mississippi River Delta
5. Petroleum and natural gas
6. The rotation of the earth
7. The recession of the moon
8. Atmospheric helium
9. Pleochroic halos
10. Population growth

Also, many fossils of plants and animals found in the supposed oldest of rocks, when compared with their living counterparts, are found to be essentially the same, in spite of presumed hundreds of millions of years of evolution. The present shellfish lingula, starfish and cockroach are examples.

Ironically, although it has been over 100 years since Darwin's time, we now have fewer examples of transitional forms than we did then. Instead of having more (as Darwin had hoped), we actually have less. This is because some of the old classic examples of evolution have been recently discarded due to new information and findings, and no new transitional forms have been found. Despite these insurmountable problems, the dauntless faith of the evolutionists persists.

According to the general theory of evolution, the basic progression leading to man occurred in the following manner:

1. Non-living matter
2. Protozoans
3. Metazoan invertebrates
4. Vertebrate fishes
5. Amphibians
6. Reptiles
7. Birds
8. Fur-bearing quadrupeds
9. Apes
10. Man

Now, as we have already established, if these things actually happened, it is perfectly logical and reasonable to expect that we should find vast numbers of transitional forms objectively preserved in the fossil record. This, however, is not the case, and the supposed transitional forms are missing in every case. Consider the following:

1. *The imagined jump from dead matter to living protozoans is a transition of true fantasy.*
2. *There is a gigantic gap between one-celled microorganisms and the high complexity and variety of the metazoan invertebrates.*
3. *The evolutionary transition between invertebrates and vertebrates is completely missing. This is absolutely incredible, since evolutionists propose 100 million years of developmental time between the two, which would have involved billions of transitional forms. Yet, not one such transitional form has been found.*
4. *There is no connecting link between amphibians and the altogether different reptiles.*
5. *There are no connecting evolutionary links between reptiles and birds. Archaeopteryx was once highly acclaimed as such a link, but has since been acknowledged by paleontologists to have been a true bird.*
6. *There are no intermediate or transitional forms leading up to man from ape-like ancestors. Fossil hominoids and hominids cited by evolutionists to demonstrate human evolution are actually fossils either of apes or men, or neither. There is no valid scientific evidence to suggest that they are fossils or animals intermediate between apes and men.*

In an attempt to explain the lack of transitional forms, some scientists have recently proposed the idea that evolution occurs via sudden large leaps, rather than through gradual small modifications. This concept, known as punctuated equilibrium, has been advanced by paleontologists Gould and Eldridge.

This concept has been termed the "hopeful monster" mechanism by Goldschmidt, who proposed that at one time a reptile laid an egg and a bird hatched from it! Creationists prefer to believe that these scientists are the ones who have laid the egg, maintaining that such ideas are pure speculation, completely devoid of any scientific evidence.

In summary, it is apparent that there is more than sufficient scientific and biblical evidence to justify complete rejection of the geological column and timetable given as science. The geologic column, which is supposedly proof of evolution, is itself actually founded upon the assumption of evolution. Thus, it is blatantly entangled in a case of circular reasoning. Important recent findings directly contradict the fundamental precepts to the geologic column and timetable. Radiometric dating techniques are based on unreliable presuppositions and, therefore, offer no scientific validity to the supposed antiquity of the earth. Hence, we conclude that the widely accepted geologic column and timetable of earth history are essential meaningless.

Ancient Earth or Young Planet?

On the other hand, there is convincing data available to support the concept of a relatively young earth. Biblical creationism and catastrophism are much better suited to the facts at hand than evolutionary uniformitarianism. The creation model, with its proper emphasis on the Genesis Flood and associated catastrophic geological events, is the only satisfactory explanation that can account for the observed complexity of geologic structures, formations, and features in the earth today. Thus, the true evidence of geology does not testify to evolution at all, but rather is a record of God's awesome power and righteous judgment on sin (The Flood).

Fossilization records present yet another serious problem for evolutionary uniformitarianism: large-scale fossilization is not occurring anywhere in the world today!

Evolutionists insist that the progression of life forms found in the fossil record from simple to complex prove the evolutionary progress of life. However, it should be pointed out that the same general progression would be expected from the hydraulic sorting action of a worldwide cataclysmic flood. Therefore, what they find when the peel back the earth's layers and look is evidence for Bible truth, not evolution, hands down. But they go on teaching their beliefs.

There are numerous specula examples of fossilization that corroborate the Genesis account of cataclysmic destruction. Animals are commonly found buried in an attitude of terror with heads arched back, mouths open, etc. We will now briefly consider a few such examples.

There are caves, fissures, and mass burial sites throughout the world that are literally packed with masses of fossils. Often times the fossils of these various animals come from widely separated and differing climactic zones, only to be thrown together in disorderly masses. Such phenomena can only be satisfactorily explained in terms of a worldwide aqueous cataclysm.

Startling evidence of the fact that a great and sudden cataclysm once struck the earth is found in the millions of mammoths and other large animals that were killed instantly in the north Polar Regions (northern Siberia and Alaska). Many of these have been found preserved whole and undamaged (except for being dead, of course) with flesh and hair intact, and in some cases, either kneeling or standing upright with food on their tongues. The eyes and red blood cells were found to be extremely well preserved, and the separation of water in the cells was only partial, which speaks of extremely sudden and sustained freezing conditions.

All uniformitarian explanations fail dismally when attempting to interpret this problem and recognize the seriousness of the threat to this theory. It is suggested that they were caught in a cold snap while swimming. This explanation, however, is obviously inadequate and simply does not fit the observed facts. Charles Darwin was also aware of the mammoths and confessed that he saw no explanation for them. There is no uniformitarian solution to this problem; the evidence unquestionably requires a sudden catastrophic explanation.

A Biblical Model of Earth History

Some creation scientists propose a possible explanation for this amazing condition—the collapse of a vast antediluvian vapor canopy that surrounded and enveloped the pre-flood world (Genesis 7:11). It is believed that such a canopy would have produced a worldwide greenhouse effect. The climate would have been mild throughout the earth with insignificant seasonal variations. No rainfall or rainbows would have existed, but rather a mist would rise from the earth that would water the whole face of the ground (Genesis 2:5-6; 8:22; 9:13).

Violent storms, such as we experience throughout the world today, would have also been precluded by this canopy (Genesis 2:5-6; Hebrews 11:7). Such a canopy would also help to explain why palm leaves, fruit trees, tropical marine crustaceans, coral reefs, and vast amounts of subtropical plant life are buried under Polar Regions. It is also believed that this vapor canopy may well have been the key factor accounting for patriarchal longevity before the flood (Genesis 5:5-27). After the flood, the ages of the various patriarchs in the Bible exhibited a steady decline:

Noah – 950 years
Sarah – 127years
Peleg – 239 years
Abraham – 175 years
Moses – 120 years
David – 70 years

Present day man — 74 years (Psalm 90:10)

Other areas of interest for the one who would like further study are:

1. Petrified logs
2. Polystrate trees (fossilized trees which extend through several layers of strata, often two feet or more in length)
3. Ephemeral markings (rain imprints, worm trails, and animal tracks found in great abundance in the fossil record)
4. Soft parts (swamp graveyards) of fossils

All of these are interesting, but the most interesting is the fact of extinctions. For many years, evolutionists have been baffled by the fact that strong, well-established groups of animals, such as dinosaurs and trilobites, suddenly disappear from the fossil record. Although their sudden departure puzzles evolutionists, creationists simply attribute their misfortune either directly or indirectly to the Genesis Flood.

Geologists have maintained that paleontology offers the most important evidence to substantiate the theory of evolution. However, as we have shown, the actual observed facts of the fossil record argue strongly against evolution and in favor of biblical creationism and catastrophes.

What About Physics?

In physics, there are problems with the evolutionary theory. We see that problems exist as we discuss the two laws of Thermodynamics. They refute evolution, and you will see why.

1. The first law of Thermodynamics is known as the Law of Energy Conservation. It states that energy can be converted from one form into another, but it can neither be created nor destroyed.

   This law teaches conclusively that the universe did not create itself. There is absolutely nothing in the present economy of natural law that could possibly account for its own origin. This scientific fact is in direct contradiction with the basic concept of naturalistic, innovation evolution. The present structure of the universe is one of conservation, not innovation, as required by the theory of   evolution.

   Although scientists cannot account for the origin of matter, they also cannot say why energy is conserved. The Bible offers an explanation. God alone can truly create. Man can only fashion preexisting materials. Since God has created from His creative works (Genesis 2:3), energy can no longer be created. The reason energy cannot be destroyed is because God is "upholding all things by the word of His power" (Hebrews 1:3). He preserves and keeps in store His creation.

Also, matter cannot be destroyed. It can be altered, but not destroyed. You can burn it, and you still have ashes. You can bury it, and you still have remains. Matter can be changed in form, but never truly done away with.

2. The second law of Thermodynamics is also a problem to the evolutionists. The second law is a law of decay. It states that every system left to its own devices tends to move; the universe is proceeding in a downward, degenerating direction of decreasing organization. Material possessions deteriorate and all living organisms eventually return to dust, a state of complete disorder.

   The second law of Thermodynamics renders the theory of evolution not only statistically highly improbably, but virtually impossible. The ironic fact is that, while they teach evolution, they cannot deny the second law of Thermodynamics. It becomes clear that they have no way of reconciling the two. No wonder our children are so confused. We are teaching them that they are evolving upward, but they are getting more decayed according to this law. This is totally contradictory.

What Does Mathematics Say?

The theory of evolution proposes that all of the highly complex structures and systems of the universe are due to the operation of purely natural and haphazard processes of nature. No external supernatural agent is needed or desired by the proponents as being self-evolving.

In direct contradiction to this philosophy, biblical creationism maintains that the innumerable, highly complex systems and intricate structures of the universe offer exceptionally strong evidence of an omniscient Creator. It is the creationist's view that the astounding degree of complexity and order found throughout the universe could never be produced by mere chance, but rather represent the handiwork of an Almighty God.

Consider the likelihood of this chance evolution of life utilizing the basic principles of mathematical probability. As Scott M. Huse put it, "Probability is simply the likelihood of an event occurring." For example, the probability of getting hit by lightning in America is about one in 15,300. The probability of winning the grand prize in an $8 million lottery game is 1 in 25 million.

Evolutionists insist that highly complex systems consisting of numerous inter-relating components can arise through a purely random and aimless process. To their way of thinking, if enough monkeys typed for long enough, eventually one of them would type a perfect, unabridged dictionary. Of course, this idea is completely nonsensical, and a brief consideration of probability statistics will reveal the absurdity and naiveté of such a viewpoint.

To illustrate, consider the likelihood of spelling the word "evolution" by randomly selecting nine letters from the alphabet. The probability is one chance in (26^9 trials [represents exponentiation]). This is equivalent to one chance in 5,429,503,680,000 (five trillion, four hundred twenty-nine billion, five hundred three million, six hundred eighty thousand)! These are rather bleak odds for such a modest request as to accidentally spell a nine-letter word – consider that![v]

You and I cannot imagine the possibility of such a thing and, mathematically, it is impossible as well.

What About Biology?

In Biology, there are literally thousands of reasons why nature is so complex that there is simply no way it could have come together by chance. Just consider the human eye, for one example.

Evolutionists are hard pressed to explain the step-by-step, chance evolution of the eye, which is characterized by a staggering complexity. Furnished with automatic aiming, automatic focusing, and automatic aperture adjustment, the human eye can function from almost complete darkness to bright sunlight, see an object the diameter of a fine hair, and make about 100,000 separate motions in an average day, faithfully affording us continuous series of color stereoscopic pictures. All of this is performed usually without complaint, and then while we sleep, it carries on its own maintenance work.

The chance of this evolving is biologically impossible. The sophistication and complexity is so precise. How could it possibly have come to being without an awesome Creator.

There is an ocean of examples to be examined in nature that is also very, very complex, and I challenge all readers to observe in life the glorious, complex creations. They are a testimony to the greatness of God, and not to an evolutionary creation. Accidents do not make masterpieces, but messes.

What About Anthropology?

The origin of man is an issue of extreme importance. The opinions of creationists and evolutionists could not be more divergent than on this particular concept. The evolutionists for many years placed their trust in the stories of many scientists who came up with pictures they thought were man's ancestors. Let's look at them.

Nebraska Man

The Nebraska Man was discovered in 1922 by Harold Cook in Pliocene deposits of Nebraska. A tremendous amount of literature was built around this supposed missing link which is alleged to have lived one million years ago. The evidence of Nebraska Man was used by evolutionists in the famous Scopes evolution trial in Dayton, Tennessee, in 1925. But what exactly was the scientific proof for Nebraska Man? The answer is, a tooth. That's right; he found a tooth! The top scientists of the world examined this tooth and appraised it as proof positive of a prehistoric race in America.

Years after the trial, the entire skeleton of the animal from which the tooth came was found. As it turns out, the tooth upon which the Nebraska Man was constructed belonged to an ancient extinct species of pig. What an embarrassment to the scientific community, and a noteworthy commentary on our human nature. Needless to say, little publicity was given to the discovered error.

A similar discovery, which was also based upon a tooth, was the Southwest Colorado Man. It is now known that this particular tooth actually belonged to a horse.

Java Man

One of the most famous of all the anthropoids is Java Man. He was discovered in 1891 by Dr. Eugene Dubois, a fervent evolutionist. He found a small piece of the top of a skull, a fragment of a left thigh bone, and three molar teeth. Although this evidence is admittedly more substantial, it is still fragmentary. Furthermore, these remnants were not found together. They were collected over a range of 70 feet. Also, they were not discovered at the same time, but over a span of one year. To further complicate matters, these remains were found in an old river bed mixed in with the bones of extinct animals. Despite all of these difficulties, evolutionists calmly assure us that Java Man lived 750,000 years ago.

Well, the experts got together and examined the fossils of Java Man's fragments. In fact, of the twenty-four European scientists who met to evaluate the find, ten said they came from an ape, seven from a man, and seven said they belonged to a no-longer-missing link. Controversy and division surrounded the discovery.

One final note regarding Java Man: another Pithecanthropus was found in Java in 1926. Typically, this discovery was also billed as a prodigious breakthrough, the missing link for sure. It turned out the be the knee bone of an extinct elephant. [vi]

Piltdown Man

The remains of Piltdown Man were allegedly discovered in 1912 by Charles Dawson, an amateur fossilologist. He produced some bones, teeth, and primitive implements, which he said he found in a gravel pit at Piltdown, Sussex, England. The remains were acclaimed by anthropologists to be about 500,000 years old. A flood of literature followed in response to this discovery with Piltdown Man being hailed in the museums and textbooks as the most wonderful of finds. Over 500 doctoral dissertations were performed on Piltdown Man.

All was well until October of 1956, when the entire hoax was exposed. Reader's Digest came out with an article, summarized from Popular Science Monthly, entitled "The Great Piltdown Hoax." Using a new method to date bones based on fluoride absorption, the Piltdown bones were fund to be fraudulent. Further critical investigation revealed that the jaw bone actually belonged to an ape that had died only 50 years previously. The teeth were filed down, and both teeth and bones were discolored with bichromate of potash to conceal their true identity. And so, Piltdown Man was built upon a deception which completely fooled all the experts who promoted him with utmost confidence.

Neanderthal Man

Neanderthal man was first discovered at about the turn of the century in a cave in the Neanderthal Valley near Dusseldorf, Germany. He was portrayed as a semierect, barrel-chested, brutish sort of fellow, an intermediary link between man and apes.

With the discovery of Neanderthal skeletons, it is now known, however, that Neanderthal Man was fully erect and fully human. In fact, his cranial capacity even exceeded that of modern man by more than 13%.

The old misconceptions about Neanderthal Man were due to two factors: first, the bias of the preprogrammed evolutionary anthropologists who reconstructed him; and second, the fact that the particular individual on whom the initial evaluation was made was crippled with osteoarthritis and rickets. Today, Neanderthal Man is classified as homo sapiens, completely human.

Lucy

Present day speculation about human evolution revolves around a group of fossils called "australopithecines," and in particular, a specimen called Lucy, a 40% complete skeleton. Lucy was discovered by D.C. Johanson in the Afar area of Ethiopia during investigations conducted from 1972 to 1977.

Scientists are still looking at Lucy and trying now to make a statement about the remains. The one thing that has already been said is that the skeleton once walked upright. They have evidence that people walked upright before Lucy. Obviously, if people walked upright before the time of Lucy, then she must be disqualified as an evolutionary ancestor. The scientists are still studying Lucy. But be leery of their perceptions, and remember the last ones.

In summary, we note the highly speculative, unreliable and imaginative nature of anthropology. To base the proposed evolutionary ancestry of man upon such fragmentary evidence is highly questionable and very misleading, especially when the evidence is not honestly presented.

Creationists contend that the only true record of man's ancestry, which began with Adam and Eve, is that which is recorded in the Bible. The Bible speaks clearly of man as a special creation, entirely unrelated to the animal kingdom by any sort of evolutionary connection (Gen. 1 and 1 Corinthians 15:39).

Summary: In short, much more needs to be studied. But man cannot be traced back further than 6-7,000 years. The science teachers will laugh at you when they hear you say that, but any other statement would be pure speculation. There is no evidence to point to any other answer. And remember, science is supposed to be based on evidence. There are no graves further back than that. There are no languages further back than that, no fossils further back than that. Writings do not go back further than that. There is no evidence back further than 6-7,000 years. Now, if anyone says any different, they are just talking. The evolutionary teaching is not only empty of proof and scientifically lacking, it is also causing tremendous damage in our world and tremendous pain. Let's examine further.

III. FALLEN FRUITS OF EVOLUTION

Evolution is a seed that brings forth fruits of hurt and destruction. I want to explain the hurts and destructive lifestyles that come with teaching that we are evolved animals.

The creation teaching of the Bible is a honorable beginning that calls on mankind to hold their head up in a joyful way, knowing that we are made in the image of God. This brings about a certain amount of responsibility.

Evolution on the other hand brings about no responsibility, but brings the feeling of acceptance of anything a person desires to do. After all, we are just elevated animals anyway (so they say). This type of thinking is what has brought on many of the destructive movements of the 1990s. The destructive movements are taking us further into the dungeon of destruction. The sad thing is that the public continues to try to look for reasons why and ways to remedy the problem without considering the foundation of evolution possibly being the problem. But if we continue to tell a child he is an elevated animal all his childhood, why are we surprised when he starts acting like an animal as an adult?

The truth lies in a statement that comes from the book of Judges in the Old Testament of the Bible. "In those days there was no king in Israel: every man did that which was right in his own eyes." (Judges 21:25)

This is the same thing as saying they had no absolute truth, therefore they did what they wanted to do and no one could tell them they were wrong, because there were no absolute truths.

If we evolved from a mud puddle, we are our own king and our own god, and we are in deep trouble.

Let's examine this problem with specifics.

1. Lawlessness and Evolution

People have always had a problem of lawlessness. Barbarianism is a result of not having the Bible or the biblical law. If you study the history of the world you will find in every society before Christ came through, before missionaries and the Bible, there was lawlessness (Barbarianism). But when the Bible came to a people, the law came. Responsibility was taught. But the biggest impact of all was the impact of the person of Jesus Christ. Jesus was kind, gentle, giving, sacrificing. He commissioned His people to keep His word and be like Him. Therefore, came civilization, civil law, etc. Think of the founding of America, for example. When Cortez and Columbus came to the New World, they found Indians in deep lawlessness. They were imprisoning each other and sacrificing their children to their gods. They were eating the flesh of young boys as if they were cows.

Cortez came to free a nation from barbaric, pagan cannibalism. His troops soon met with one horrendous sight after another: human hearts that had been cut out of living prisoners found nailed to temple walls; pyramid-style temples covered with human blood; bodies of men and boys without arms and legs; human skulls regularly arranged in piles; gnawed human bones piled in houses and streets; wooden houses build with grating jammed full of captives being fattened up for sacrifice; pagan priests matted with dried human blood, covered the temple steps where frenzied hoards ate their bodies; devotees eating the fresh carcasses of those who were sacrificed, roasted human arms, legs and heads; warriors eating the corpses of those they slew in battle; etc.

This was a result of their religion; they believed that all the universe was one, and that people were just of the universe. They believed that the sun god needed human blood to live, and that the Aztecs were responsible to feed him the blood he needed daily.

This is an example of a people without the Bible and without the person of Jesus Christ as their example. But the Bible came through missionaries and through the Great Commission of Christ in Matthew 28:18-20: "Go ye therefore, and teach all nations, baptizing them in the name of the Father, and the Son, and of the Holy Ghost: Teaching them to observe all things whatsoever I have commanded you: and lo, I am with you always, even unto the end of the world. Amen."

Therefore, the believers in creation and the biblical scriptures have been going ever since. When they get where they are going, they are teaching Christ and bringing love and law with that teaching. Really, they are bringing with them the personality of Jesus Christ, and therefore, bringing the person of God to the people. God is good and brings civilized law, kindness, giving instead of taking, and sacrifice *for* people rather than selfishness and sacrifice *of* people.

Some may say God is a taker. But God has created us to do for us and in the history of the world, we can see that all God asks of man is for man's good. God gets nothing from man. God is very good.

But lawlessness comes to a people when they are away from God. Lawlessness is a result of no Supreme Being to answer to. When the person of Christ and His Father are removed from a society, men look for purpose without God. Therefore, they begin to live only to gratify self. Lust and flesh become the gods of man. Really, man becomes his own god and the reason to live becomes pleasure. Therefore, man seeks to satisfy self at *any* expense. And most of the time it is at the expense of others – those who are not big enough to stop them. This is really Barbarianism, not law.

An important bit of information needs to be inserted here. The Bible is the source of man's conscience. Without the Bible, men cannot distinguish between right and wrong. There is no conscience without the Bible. Therefore, we are removing the Bible from our children and in fact removing absolutes and removing the conscience from their hearts. The conscience is the voice that cries out from within when considering doing something that is wrong. This voice shouts, "Stop, stop, it's wrong!" But think, if the Bible is not the absolute truth, how can we say what is right or wrong? If the new generations are absent from biblical truth, they are absent from the voice that cries, it's wrong or it's right. No Bible, no conscience. That's why one teen can kill his classmate, brother, or mother and not even be burdened about it. The conscience has been removed!

Another very important point. If the Bible is not the standard for right and wrong, then what is the standard? The standard becomes different to everyone. Where is absolute truth? That is why in the 1990s, people continue to challenge basic foundational truths. They continue to ask by what standard we measure right or wrong. I think you understand the dilemma brought on by the evolution foundation. This teaching is destroying our basis for conscience, and all basic truths. How can we survive such a tragedy?

Some have tried to say that the creation part is not totally acceptable but the rest of the Bible we accept. But that only lasts a little while. Then someone else challenges another area. Then before you know it, the total Bible has been labeled questionable. Before you know it the Bible is totally shunned as truth. Then our leaders decide they need to develop truths. Then others challenge those truths and the truths change. This, of course, develops a slippery, uncertain foundation and is disastrous for society.

This will get worse unless the Bible is absolute truth. This will get worse unless Christ is taught and the personality of God is given to society. You see, there is no freedom for any if Christ is not the God of society. There is no stability for a society without the Bible as absolute truth. The problem with society today is that we continue to take away those motivations of inner conscience. If we continue to disregard the Bible and teach our future generations that are kin to the beast of the field and not to God, what kind of people do we expect them to be?

You see, we are taking away the source for good, godly people in the world. Therefore, fear of being caught is the only motivation for doing good. Then we fill our jails and build bigger jails, etc. We continue to have budget problems because we continue to need more and more policemen to sit on every corner and remind them of the punishment for doing wrong. But if we develop that love of Christ into our people, then we do not have a jail crowding problem.

A prime example is public school without God and Christian school with God and godly, Christlike principles being taught. I rest my case. A people motivated by their hearts are motivated by a powerful force: love for God.

Let me ask you a question. If you were a farmer and you wanted a good crop for your table, and you decided to build a canopy over your fields to shield them from the sun because you didn't like the fact that it hurt your eyes and burned your skin if you stayed out there too long, what do you think would happen to the hopes of a good crop! I rest my case!

2. Abortion and Evolution

Abortion is a product of this "no God" thinking. There was a time when life was looked at as something very wonderful and dear. We were to save a life at all costs. Our doctors would even state an oath to save a life with all their might, but this was during a time when the Bible was the prominent teacher of society. God was our Creator and we were made by Him and in His image, therefore we exist and have our being. We are a part of Him. Therefore, we are a special creation. Life in man is an extension of God. Genesis 1:27, "So God created man in His own image, in the image of God created he him; male and female created he them." Genesis 2:7, "And the Lord God formed man of the dust of the ground, and breathed into his nostrils the breath of life; and man became a living soul."

This is the teaching that brought a respect for human life. But the teaching of evolution is simply an evolutionary picture of raising up out of a mud pit. The difference is very extreme. The results are also very extreme.

As mentioned earlier, many will remember being taught in school that an embryo develops in its mother's womb. They said the embryo goes through a fish stage with gill slits, etc., and other evolutionary stages until it becomes human. In other words, the idea is that, as the embryo develops, it passes through all the evolutionary stages reflecting its ancestry. This theory of "embryonic recapitulation" was first proposed by a man named Ernest Haeckel. Not many people realize that this whole theory was an intentional deception. I quote, "But it still remains true that, in attempting to prove his law, Haeckel resorted to a series of dishonest distortions in making his illustrations. Branding them as dishonest is not too harsh, since Haeckel mentions where he originally procured some of his drawings without mentioning the alterations he made," (creation Research Society 1969 Annual, Volume 6, Number 1, June 1969, p.28).

Eventually, Ernest Haeckel admitted this fraud, but the deplorable aspect is that this theory is still taught in many universities, schools and colleges throughout the world. Admittedly, evolutionists who have kept up with the latest writings know that this view is wrong and refrain from teaching it in their classes. However, in most of the popular school textbooks and reading materials this view is still promulgated in various forms, often very subtly.

As people accepted that the child developing in a mother's womb was just an animal reflecting its evolutionary ancestry there was less and less problem about destroying it. As evolutionary ideas became more accepted, the easier it became to accept abortion. In fact, some abortion clinics in America have taken women aside to explain to them that what is being aborted is just an embryo in the fish stage of evolution, and that the embryo must not be thought of as human. These women are being fed outright lies.

Abortion was in existence before Darwin, but evolution gave abortion the respect that it needed. Really, evolution gave atheism a respectability as well.

Accepting the God of Creation tells us what life is all about. We know that God is the life giver. We know that life has meaning and purpose, and we know that humans are created in the image of God, therefore, are of great value and significance. God made man so that He could relate to us, love us and pour out His blessing on us, and so that we could love Him in return.

It must be understood that our view of everything is affected and altered by what we believe about our beginnings. As the creation foundations are removed, we see that the views that give life and respect for life are also removed. We must understand the connection between creation and abortion. If infants in the womb are not people but animals, what's wrong with aborting an animal that is not wanted? You see, we take our animals to the local animal shelter and if they are not wanted, we put them to sleep. This practice came into being as a result of how we view animals. Animals are viewed as having no eternal souls. But man was created in the image of God and has an eternal soul. They have been taught that man is just an elevated animal with no eternal soul, and it has become easy to just put to death what is not wanted or convenient. Therefore, the foundation of abortion!

3. Homosexuality and Evolution

Homosexuality is today primarily fed by the evolutionary thought of evolving to new forms. If we have no God and no law giver above man, then we can make our own rules, and if we have a desire to defile ourselves with mankind, we have the right to do so.

Also, homosexuality is thought of in some circles as just another process of evolutionary progression. They feel that man has gone through many different changes. Therefore, this is just another change in the history of man. But homosexuality (or sodomy as the Bible calls it) has been around for many centuries and in many cultures. Homosexuality is not new. This is just another destructive mode of man rearing its ugly head once again to exalt itself against the design of God. It is fueled by the desire for fleshly, self-gratification. Such people are seeking this gratification in increasing measure to take them to new heights of ecstasy. Under the spell of the great deceiver, Satan, they do not see that the higher they go, the deeper they sink into sin.

Those who submit to this sin of sodomy are looking for fulfillment in fleshly desires because they believe that they have no other purpose to live except to satisfy the flesh and its cravings. In essence, live for today because (they believe) there is no God, the Bible is not true, and therefore, there will be no judgement. Evolution teaches that we are animals anyway, so we may as well experience all this life has to offer with as many other animals as possible. It is easy to see how homosexuality is given respect and believability by evolution.

Sadly, it is not just atheists or agnostics who buy into such lies as evolution and homosexuality. The sin of homosexuality is becoming more prominent in the camps of professing believers in God. These commit just as fatal an error, by misinterpreting Scripture and distorting God's design by claiming His approval for their "lifestyle choice" (sin). Without erasing or distorting Bible truth, sodomy would be sin – totally an unacceptable lifestyle. This story of sin and perversion has appeared many times throughout the pages of history, but every time it was seen just prior to a people destroyed themselves.

4. Nazism and Evolution

Nazism is also a state in the evolutionary spiral. Much has been written about one of Fascism's more famous sons, Adolph Hitler. His treatment of the Jews may be attributed, at least in part, to his belief in evolution. P. Hoffman, in *Hitler's Security* (Pergamon, 1979, p. 264), said, "Hitler believed in struggles as a Darwinian principle of human life that forced people to try to dominate all others; without struggle they would perish. Even in his own defeat in April 1945, Hitler expressed his faith in the survival of the stronger and declared the Slavic peoples to have proven themselves the stronger."

Sir Arthur Keith, the well-known evolutionist, explains how Hitler was only being consistent in what he did to the Jews – he was applying the principles of Darwin's evolution. In *Evolution and Ethics* (New York, Pyman, 1947, p. 28) he said, "To see evolutionary measures and tribal morality being applied vigorously to the affairs of a great modern nation, we must turn again to the Germany of 1942. We see Hitler devoutly convinced that evolution produces the only real basis of a national policy... The means he adopted to secure the destiny of his race and people was organized slaughter, which has drenched Europe in blood... Such conduct is highly immoral as measured by every scale of ethics, yet Germany justified it; it is consonant with tribal or evolutionary morality. Germany has reverted to the tribal past, and is demonstrating to the world, in their naked ferocity, the methods of evolution." Only the strong survive. This is the upward progression of the races as it is in the animal realm.

5. Racism and Evolution

Stephen J. Gould in *Natural History* (April 1980, p. 144) said, "Recapitulation (the evolutionary theory which postulates that a developing embryo in its mother's womb goes through evolutionary stages, such as the fish stage, etc., until it becomes human) provided a convenient focus for the pervasive racism of white scientists; they looked to the activities of their own children for comparison with normal, adult behavior in lower races." Gould also concludes that the term "mongoloid" became synonymous with mentally defective people because it was believed that the Caucasian race was more highly developed than the Mongoloid. Therefore, some thought that a mentally defective child was really a throwback to a previous stage in evolution. The leading American paleontologist of the first half of the twentieth century, Henry Fairfield Osborne, adds fuel to the fire with his believe that, "The Negroid stock is even more ancient than the Caucasian and Mongolian. The standard of intelligence of the average adult Negro is similar to that of the eleven-year-old of the species Homo Sapiens" (*Natural History*, April 1980, p. 129).

If the evolutionary view is not removed from the teaching of our education system as the truth of our beginning, racism will worsen instead of improve.

Racism in America

America has been imploding with the issue of racism for over a hundred years. America has constantly made attempts to resolve the struggle between the African American community and the rest of America. America is a melting pot of different people groups, but the more we try to fix this racism problem, the worse it gets.

Programs in the United States, programs that open doors to the African American community, have been hampered by a mindset created by the teaching of evolution. The American classroom continues to teach a thought that one race is greater than another, and that one group of people is more developed than another. If this offends you, you do not understand the evolutionary thought. Evolution teaches survival of the fittest, and that one group of people will outperform another. This is at the core of evolutionary thought. This is at the heart of Darwin's teaching, and cannot be denied. Therefore, when we allow our children to be taught the theory of evolution, we are establishing a mindset of racism. We are crippling a race of people by expecting less of them. The facts are the facts! And, yes, our politicians have used racism in America as a political football. The

African American has been promised many handouts and many helps, but in the long run, they have become dependent on the charity of others and, in turn, have been crippled by lack of expectations. A great example of this is the rage that is being seen concerning the voter laws that have been changed after the election of 2020. These new laws would require all American registered voters to have valid IDs in order to vote. Those who are upset about these laws are declaring that they discriminate against the African American, because they say the African American cannot get an ID like everyone else. This is degrading toward the African American community, as the politicians do not believe that they need to be required to do have an ID. This is really true racism, and would not be possible without the mindset created by evolutionary teaching. Some would say that this is just politics, but the validity of their argument is not rooted in truth, and would not be possible without a Darwin mindset in America.

The best thing that could happen to the African American community is to treat them the same way as every other American or every other immigrant group in America. All Americans are immigrants except for Native Americans, and have come to America from various parts of the world to better their families and the future of their families. It would be the greatest thing for the African American community to be treated like all other Americans, rather than a group of people that needs to be carried constantly. But this author is simply pointing out that this would not be possible without the mindset of evolutionary thought.

In truth, evolutionary teaching is a tool to enslave the group called the African American.

6. Drugs and Evolution

Most people would not consider evolution involved in any way with the drug abuse problem. However, the following letter of testimony from a man in Western Australia shows clearly this relationship. (Taken from Ken Ham's book, *The Lie*. P. 87.)

"At school, the theory of evolution was presented in such a way that none of us ever doubted it was scientific fact. Although the school was supposedly Christian, the biblical account of creation was presented as a kind of romantic fiction, not intended to convey truths about God, man or the cosmos. As a result, I assumed the Bible was not scientific, and therefore practically of little or not use.

It never occurred to me that evolution was only an assumption – a concept in someone's head – and I regret to say that I wasn't sufficiently interested to go check out the so-called facts for myself. I assumed that reliable people had already done that.

After I left school, I began to put into practice the assumption and presuppositions I'd picked up during childhood. My naïve belief in evolution had three important practical consequences:

1. It strongly encouraged me to look to drugs as an ultimate source of comfort.

2. It led me to the conclusion that God, if He was around at all, was a very distant and impersonal figure, separated from humanity by very great distances of space and time.

3. It led me to increasingly abandon the moral values I had been taught at home, because when man is viewed as an arbitrary by-product of Time+Matter+Chance, there is no logical reason for treating men or women as objects of dignity and respect, since in principle they are no different from the animals, trees, and rocks from which they supposedly came.

I want to elaborate on just one point, the great faith in dope that came as a result of being convinced that evolution was fact. After leaving school, I became increasingly susceptible to drugs. Drug-taking seemed to me to make sense, because in principle it fit what I'd been taught abut the nature and origin of man. From chemical reactions has thou come, and unto chemicals thou shalt return. And so I did.

My faith in drugs as a source of comfort and creativity was almost unbreakable even after ten years of total devastation, during which job, personality and relationships had fallen apart. Even after I came to Christ, I still continued using drugs and feeling strongly drawn to using them, until some Christians had pointed out the truth about man's nature, origin and destiny as recounted in Genesis. It was only when I perceived the truth of this, that my private love of drugs was completely and voluntarily abandoned. I now know that my hope is in the Person of Jesus Christ, and in Him only. It's no longer a platitude, but a living reality. I'm free, and it is the truth which has made me free—free even from any desires for dope, free from the compelling faith I once had in chemicals as a result of believing in a lie—the lie of evolution. I appeal to you parents and teachers, to reexamine the evidence as I have done."

Drug use in an escape means that is being used when a person has no purpose and is frustrated with life as they see it. Drugs take them away from reality.

If we are an evolutionary accident and there is no God, if we have no purpose, and if when we finish here, we return to the dust with no afterlife, we are men most miserable. Therefore, we need something to reach for to give us some reason to live, such as drugs, but not just drugs. This type of thinking produces all sorts of dependencies.

We as evolutionary creatures must find some reason to live here. Therefore, there is a great search going on across the world for something to live for, some humanistic filler of the void in life.

As a pastor I continually visit the homes of young men and women who have turned to drugs, alcohol, sex and other fillers of the void in their lives. I continue to ask them about their purpose in life, their ambitions, and their dreams. The one problem they seem to have is none of the above. They lie in the bed. They will not go try to get a job. They walk wherever they go if someone will not take them. They have lost their purpose. They feel as if they are here for a brief time and they have no significance at all in this world, no ambition, no purpose, no dreams, no reason for existence, and there they turn to drugs, alcohol, sex or any other reasons for purpose. This is without question a direct result of evolutionary theft. Evolutionary teaching has stolen their purpose. We continue to be faced with a group of parents who will not even take care of their own children, let alone be responsible for or to others. Where are they? They ignore parental responsibility. They are looking for something for *themselves* rather than sacrificing for others. This is totally away from God's Son's sacrificial example.

Let me just say, if we continue to close our eyes to the poison that is being fed to our children's minds every day, we will continue to have a sicker and sicker generation of graduates.

The American taxpayer will carry the load of drug abuse in America. The Office of the National Drug Control Policy requested for 2021 the amount of $34.6 billion to fight the issue of drug addiction in America, in addition to the $1.2 billion requested by the Department of Defense for counter drug operations at home and abroad.

7. Euthanasia and Evolution

We are facing in the 1990's an extremely devastating teaching. Dr. Death is the greatest example of what I am trying to alert our nation to in this book. Dr. Death, as he is called, is continually assisting people in their suicidal desires. If you have any wisdom or understanding at all, you must see the relation of Dr. Death and his beliefs founded in evolutionary teaching. He is proclaiming that a person has the right to take his own life if he so desires. The abortionist shouts about a woman's right to make choices about what's in her body. The Euthanasia promoter shouts about the right to live or die. All totally ignore God and creation. All continually ignore all other people involved and just desire to please self. These are the bold examples of selfishness, the total opposite of Jesus' personality.

The danger of Euthanasia is, of course, the future execution of the aged, the mentally handicapped, and those who cannot add to the benefit of society. The promoters of such a practice will shout that it will not go that far, but consider the past records of that group. They are becoming increasingly motivated by profit. Yes, money. The abortion industry is money-motivated. The Euthanasian success will eliminate society from a tremendous financial load of taking care of the aged and the sick. See what I mean?

Also, I would like you to recognize this Euthanasia teaching for what it is. This is nothing more than Hitler's teaching just dressed in another uniform. Hitler tried to eliminate the Jews because he said they were weak and needed to be eliminated.

Examine communism. If humans cannot help the state, what happens to them?

You see, Christianity is where we get our teaching about love of parents and sacrificing for others. Life is important, a gift from God. Man is created in the image of God, different from a dog.

Evolution is the direct opposite. Let's speculate for a minute:

Think about the future clinics set up in America to do away with those who do not desire to live anymore. Some would say it couldn't happen in America. Think about the abortion industry and then think about euthanasia and tell me it couldn't' happen! It's all a product of evolutionary poison fed into the minds of new graduates. Think of having a child and the child having birth defects and the doctors, hospitals or the insurance providers refusing to treat the child. Think of your aged mother being refused treatment because of her age or condition.

Can you see the dilemma shaping up for you and me?

You see, the value of life is directly related to evolution. Our present and future happiness hinges on these beliefs. If we do not see man as an extension of God, the future is black and full of troubles.

8. The World Troubles and Evolution

The world has been very cursed by the attitude of evolution, (man is God). Evolution is not listed in the public arena as a reason for many of the troubles in our past history worldwide. But in the wars of our world's past, we can say that all of them were fueled by men who were self-centered and proud. That is the opposite of Christ and Christianity. Many people will try to blame God for the many wars of the world. And I know that it is true that many of the world's countries have been filled with war over religion. But let's not blame God and the person of Jesus Christ with pride and personal wars raged in the name of religion. If you truly know the life of Christ, you know that Jesus did not order nor encourage war at all. The Old Testament was filled with war, but Christ and Christianity were to be filled with loving enemies and doing good to those who despitefully use you.

Some will try to say that God is not peace loving, and for those people we will pray and we will realize that they do not know the whole story. They are usually just looking for a reason not to yield to God and call him Lord. Therefore, they continue to say that they want no part of God because of the trouble caused by religion. This reminds me of a man I once was inviting to come to know Jesus Christ. This man informed me that he wanted nothing to do with a God that caused wars. This poor man didn't know much about God. He was in one of the wars and saw a lot of pain. He said the pain was caused by God. God doesn't cause war. A good example of this in our times is abortion doctors being killed by people saying that God told them to do it. This is, of course, not God's directing, but they continue to say so. Therefore, many people think God is a Person who tells people to kill. In the Old Testament this was true. But we are no to model ourselves after the personality of Christ, and the fruit of His Spirit is love, joy, and peace, etc.

The real reason for war is selfish pride. Someone is trying to take something in a self-centered move and others must stop them. This, of course, is a selfish move motivated by living for self or lust of the flesh. Therefore, lust of the flesh is a product of evolutionary thought. When people worship false gods or themselves as god, they live for flesh or self-gratification. Therefore, they continue to act as if they are animals fighting for survival.

Let's compare the French Revolution with the American Revolution. The French Revolution was motivated and totally fueled by self-promotion and a no-God attitude. Therefore, the French Revolution was a devastating and cruel revolution, not like the American Revolution at all. The American Revolution was a group of Christian gentlemen in a war. The cruelty of war was not a major issue at all. But the French Revolution was filled with extreme stories of cruelty such as the removal of heads by guillotine, etc. The French Revolution, we are told by historians, was staged by a violent birth of pure, socialistic humanism. This was a start contrast to the American Revolution, which was founded firmly upon God and bathed in prayer.

Before the American Revolution, the Colonies experienced a great spiritual awakening called the Great Awakening One. This was fueled by the preaching of men like John and Charles Wesley and George Whitefield. Their preaching was based on God as Creator and Jesus as His Son. They were preaching the person of Jesus Christ and His teachings. Therefore, the men of that day became men of godly character such as George Washington, John Adams, etc.

England was also under the influence of the same teaching. Therefore, the American Revolution and the French Revolution were so different. Even the American Civil War, as bad as it was, still was buffeted by Christian people who held back much of the devastation that would have occurred otherwise.

On the other hand, World Wars I and II were both started and fueled by evolutionary thought.

These two wars, as well as the Korean and Vietnam conflicts, were all the product of either fascism or communism which are finitely founded on atheism and humanism (man is god).

We can clearly see that the trail of evolution and humanism is filled with selfishness and pain, i.e., the French Revolution, the Holocaust, the cruelty of communism, etc. This is in the past. But the present is filled with abortion, homosexuality, Aids, racism and many other destructions of our day. What kind of fruit do you think is in store for us in the future with the mass teaching of evolution and the indoctrination of humanism (man is god) being taught to our children daily? I hope you can see this wave of destruction now present and still building in power.

Foundations of Modern Science

Science has been and still is a friend of Christianity. The study of God's created world is a great thing and will glorify God when done in truth and with the premise that He exists. "The heavens declare the glory of God; and the firmament showeth his handiwork" (Psalm 19:1). The people of the 90s have a hard time seeing science as the friend of Christianity and God. We have a hard time seeing how God could possibly be glorified in science. But it is true. Science was once a tremendous friend of God. Or maybe I need to say, God was a tremendous friend of science. Let me explain.

At one time science was primarily the study of the stars. There was very little known about nature or natural order, etc.

The Ancient Greeks, through Aristotle, thought that the earth was the center of everything. The Greeks thought the stars were so wonderful that man needed to worship them. They worshiped the creation instead of the creator. Mankind was in such dismay of nature and fear of nature they felt as if they needed to worship the elements in order to ensure that the elements would be good to them. For example, they knew that they needed to remove the sin and to get the sun to bless them they would offer sacrifice to the sun god. Therefore, they worshiped the creation rather than the creator. They had a hard time separating the creator from the creation. In the light of this time of science, science suffered extreme darkness and stagnations.

There were a few ancient men who from time to time would perform some magnificent feats of inventing or grasp some great bit of wisdom. The Egyptians built the pyramids. The Egyptians and Babylonians both developed calendars. Both groups, however, believed in astrology, the confused idea that the destinies of men are ruled by the stars, rather than by the Creator of the stars. They never understood that the stars are controlled by natural forces and rational laws of nature that were established by God. And this God for His purpose can invent whatever He desires. They worshiped nature itself as a god. This nature worship prevented them from discovering the general principles that have made science possible, and thus their science was merely a series of trial and errors. The Asian people, with their stress on man being at one with nature, and with their system of astrology, was similarly unable to develop scientific principles, although they developed some technology, such a printing and paper.

Aristotle gave them a basic foundational for their science that just wouldn't take them anywhere. What they tried to do just wouldn't come together because of the foundation principles. Their premise or philosophy was that the earth or man was the center of the universe. They believed that the sun rotated around the earth, and that man was one with nature. They couldn't separate God and creation. They taught that there were many gods. These basic premises were flawed and just didn't work. But for many years they were the basic foundation of science. Therefore, they just were not very productive.

Let's think for a moment, and notice that their philosophy is very similar to the teaching today in science, and in religions (New Age).
1. *We are one with nature (New Age).*
2. *Man is at the center of importance, not God.*
3. *There are many gods.*
4. *It doesn't matter which one you serve.*
5. *God is everywhere and in everything.*
6. *Nature is worshiped as god.*

The foundational Creation philosophy found in the Bible came to man and gave him a whole different way of looking at everything, a biblical way.

1.   *The sun is at the center and earth revolves around it.*

2.   *There is one God and He is our Creator*

3.   *There is order to everything and our God is a God of order.*

4.   *Since there is one God and He is faithful, every action set in motion by Him is always faithful. His word is the source of knowledge*

Therefore, we were able to study the body of man with the premise of the English Bible. Technology took off with the foundation of these premises, by the English Bible. This began to take place in the middle of the 1300s. John Wycliffe put the Bible into the English-speaking people's language and then science began its greatest hour. Ken Ham calls it from Darkness to Light in his book, *Genesis and the Decay of the Nations*. Let us go back in time to a man who was very concerned about foundations, to a man who had no doubts concerning the infallibility of the Bible and the foundational importance of Genesis. On October 31, 1517, Martin Luther nailed his 95 theses to the door and marked the beginning of the Reformation. Martin Luther was a man concerned about foundations. He pleaded with the church of his day to have the Word of God as their basis for truth. He recognized that creation was a basis and vital to all truth. The reformation he spearheaded was the beginning of man's emergence from the Dark Ages.

This was the birth of modern science. Modern science was the greatest hour of science. Modern science has taken man into an age of wonder in the discoveries that have been made since the Bible became the foundation. Those of us schooled from 1960-1990 have a hard time believing that the Bible and science were even in the same camp, but truly they were. And this united pair brought on science and man's greatest hour.

At the same time of the Pilgrims' departure for the New World, England was beginning to come into some glory in science. By the coming of the English Bible came wisdom from God and then God began to work through His people who were reading His book. The greatest of all ancient books was returned to the people as the central textbook and many discoveries began to spring forth.

Francis Bacon (1561-1626), the English philosopher who played a big role in formulating the principles of modern scientific method, explained the connection between the Protestant Reformation and modern science this way:

"...when it pleased God to call the church of Rome to account for their degenerate manners and ceremonies, and the same time it was ordained by the Divine Providence that there should attend withal a renovation and a new spring of all other knowledges."

1. *People learned to search for truth for themselves, both in the Scriptures and in nature, rather than to depend on the pagan authorities and the church leaders.*

2. *As people turned to the Scriptures, they learned that God created the universe, that He is separate from the universe, and that He established reasonable, orderly laws which nature obeys.*

3. *The early scientists began to search for the laws that God had established so they could understand nature and control it for the good of man, as God commanded in Genesis 1:28.*

4. *Once countries such as Holland and England became Protestant, scientists had a place where they could carry on their work free from the persecution of the Catholic Church leaders. Most of the early scientists were Protestant, though others were Catholics who dared to question the official church dogma on scientific issues. Many were devout Christians. Because they believed the Bible, they had a good understanding of basic truths about the universe, for the Author of the Bible is the Creator of the universe.*

5. *People taught by the Bible felt a responsibility to use their God-given*

talents to find ways to help other people. Science gave them a very important tool for benefiting mankind.

The big breakthrough for modern science came in 1543. It was then Nicholas Copernicus (1473-1543), a polished astronomer, published his book, The Revolutions of Celestial Spheres. He had worked with practically the same information the other astronomers possessed, but he used his own observations and the reasoning powers God had given him rather than blindly following the ideas of Aristotle and the schoolmen. This enabled him to propose a new way of understanding the universe. Copernicus said that the planets, including the earth, revolved around the sun, and that the earth is not the motionless body about which everything else in the universe moves. Today we accept the heliocentric (sun centered) approach without question, but in Copernicus's era, it was the beginning of a scientific revolution, for until that time the universe had been understood as being geocentric (earth centered). A whole new approach would be required in physics, vastly different from Aristotle's.

Taking "pleasure in the exalted contemplation of the divine mechanism," derived by the wisest Creator, "Kepler discovered the three laws of planetary motion. The first law states that planets go around the sun, and the third explains the relationship between the times of the revolutions of the planets about the sun and their distances from that body.

Kepler then gave all the glory to God for the divine wisdom.

Then Galileo Galilei (1564-1642) was born in Pisa, Italy, twenty-one years after the death of Copernicus. He lived about the same time as Kepler. When he was nineteen, he observed a bronze lamp swinging from an arch in the Pisa Cathedral. This would lead him to develop the law of the pendulum and to invent a machine for calculating the rate of a person's pulse. Many other observations were given science by this man in his life.

Then Sir Isaac Newton (1642-1717), a brilliant and godly man, a devout Christian, contributed more to scientific progress on mankind than any other single individual before or since. Standing on the shoulders of Galileo, Kepler, Copernicus, Newton of the physical universe, Newton was first concerned about the force that kept the planets in orbit.

Newton's first rule of reasoning was, "We are to admit no more causes of natural things than such as are both true and sufficient to explain their appearances."

Newton discovered the Universal Law of Gravitation: Every particle of matter in the universe attracts every other particle of matter with a force directly proportional to its quantity of matter, and decreasing as the square of the distance increases.

With this single mathematical law, Newton stated a truth about every particle of matter in the physical universe.

Then there were a host of other discoveries by other scientists that we will not in this study observe for you but challenge you to do a study of your own. However, by getting away from Aristotle's concept and coming to the Biblical Creator mode of thought, came wisdom and a beginning in the area of science. Later other discoveries followed from this foundation as well as from these valuable discoveries. The wonder of all these and other discoveries is that they took place by a revival in the return to God's word as the authority of life.

Modern science took a turn for the worse in the mid-1800s. Darwin and a host of others came forth with their ideas that were not biblical. Darwin and others dealt a very damaging blow to the field of science.

Darwin's theory is now taught as facts learned through observing and studying evidence. There never was, and has never been any fact or basis for evolution teaching. A shameful devastation has been done by all who try to teach and preach this in science when theory is not science at all.

Science's greatest hour has been without question from 1500 up through the 1990s. We are still running on the momentum gained by the Bible foundation of the last 350 years. But we are now beginning to see a blindness set in. The evolution theory is changing, with opinion after opinion coming further for all the time. But the push is still on to promote and accept. We are really just returning to a society of self-motivation a no-God view. This is not new, but simply a return to the Dark Ages.

The challenge that is the real problem is not among scientists, however. The real damage is when Christians compromise and accept the faulty foundation. From 1850-1998 the confusion has been growing worse and worse. Christians are being influenced by the public schools, media teaching and every aspect that is built on the evolutionary premise. How can we go to the schools and colleges and hear it all the time and not fall for it? The only way is through study after study of truth, the continual proclamation of truth.

We must study to show ourselves approved, a workman that need not be ashamed. We must know the facts and share the facts. We must question the teachers and scientists. We must know the questions to ask and we must know the answers as well. God will bless you if you desire to become informed. God bless you in your endeavor. Be God's salt and light and stop the decay of the truth.

Remember science's greatest hour was when science was based on creation. Science really began to move only when they discovered biblical truths and began to apply them to scientific studies.

Please understand. I know that science has made many wonderful discoveries between 1850 and 2021, but those discoveries are a result of the creation foundation given to them after 1300.

IV. SCIENCE AND SCRIPTURE: FRIENDS OR FOES?

The Bible is very good at stating its friends and foes. Science was never intended to be a foe of the Bible. The science of our day has become an enemy of God because of those who have decided they did not need the Bible to find truth. They also have fallen into the trap of thinking that the world and its appearance of age is really old. You see, when God created man He did not create a baby, but a full grown man. When God created a fruit tree, He created a fruit tree with the appearance of age. Also, the flood did an amazing job of changing the appearance of the earth's crust. If a person wanted to say the earth was old by erosion or the appearance of age, that would be his choice. But God left enough evidence in the fossil record, historical record, etc., to provide an inquiring mind plenty of reason to accept His word if that person first read the word and second if that person really wanted to know the truth.

The Bible in its explanation of Creation has no room for error. Anyone disagreeing with the Bible is a disaster waiting for a place to happen.

There are no areas of compromise about Creation and God. Many have tried to compromise and say that God used evolution to create. But the Bible is very specific and man must understand the importance of the Creation foundation. Every area of our life is affected by what we believe about where we come from – marriage, family, child bearing, the sin of man, our need for Jesus and the gospel story of redemption. I think you understand that the Creation story is the foundation for the rest of the Bible as well as the foundation for every other area of our lives. We can see the confusion and destruction taking place in the lives of those who reject the biblical foundation. Let's look at a few biblical statements that God gave us to make sure that we had no other ideas about where we came from and our greatest needs.

I. The Bible and the findings of science do not conflict.

a. God links together the written word and the message from His creation.

Psalms 19:1-7
    1. The heavens declare the glory of God; and the firmament sheweth his handiwork. 2. Day unto day uttereth speech, and night unto night sheweth knowledge. 3. There is no speech nor language, where their voice is not heard. 4. Their line is gone out through all the earth, and their words to the end of the world...

Job 12:7-10

    Job recognizes the fact that even the animals can teach how God is related to all life; 7. But ask now the beasts, and they shall teach thee; and the fowls of the air, and then shall tell thee: 8. Or speak to the earth, and it shall teach thee: and the fishes of the sea shall declare unto thee. 9. Who knoweth not in all these that the hand of the LORD hath wrought this? 10. In whose hand is the soul of every living thing, and the breath of all mankind.

Romans 1:19, 20

Here again, God judges man for refusing to read His message in the creation around him: 19...Because that which may be known of God is manifest in them; for God hath shewed it unto them. 20: For the invisible things of him from the creation of the world are clearly seen, being understood by the things that are made, even his eternal power and Godhead; so that they are without excuse.

Matthew 6:26-34

Behold the fowls of the air: for they sow not, neither do they reap, nor gather into barns; yet your heavenly Father feedeth them. Are ye not much better than they? 28...Consider the lilies of the field...30...if God so clothe the grass...shall he not much more clothe you...?

b. God's nature is such that He could not be guilty of presenting to us conflicting messages in the Bible and Creation.

Numbers 23:19

God speaking through Balaam to Balak: God is not a man, that He should lie...

Titus 1:2

Paul, too, speaks of God Who cannot lie.

1 Corinthians 14:33

For God is not the author of confusion, but of peace...

2. The fact that God is Creator is taught all through the Scriptures.

Because this is true, to refuse to accept God's creative work is to place oneself above God's Word and refuse all of Scripture and call God a liar.

Here are sample passages that refer to specific acts of creation that are cited.

Genesis 1:1

In the beginning God created the heaven and the earth.

Exodus 20:11

For in six days the LORD made heaven and earth, the sea, and all that in them is, and rested the seventh day.

Deuteronomy 4:32

...Since the day that God created man upon the earth...

1 Samuel 2:8 (Hannah praying)

...For the pillars of the earth are the LORD's, and he hath set the world upon them.

Malachi 2:10

Have we not all one father? Hath not one God created us?

Why do we deal treacherously every man against his brother, by profaning the covenant of our fathers?

3. God's creative work took place in six solar days.

Genesis 1:5, 8, 13, 19, 23, 31

God especially speaks of the evening and the morning of each of the six days.

Genesis 1:9-13 and 20-27

God created plants on the third day, and animal life on the fifth and sixth days. Many plants need life on the fifth and sixth days. Many plants need insects and animals to pollinate them so that they can reproduce. If a long interval existed before there was pollination,

Matthew 19:4 (Jesus speaking to the Pharisees)

Genesis 1:6

much of the plant life would die before it reproduced.

Exodus 20:8-11

God set aside the seventh day as a remembrance of His resting after six days of creation.

4. God on many occasions has worked suddenly and completely; He is not limited to working over a long period of time.

a. God spoke many things into existence.

Genesis 1:3

And God said, Let there be light: and there was light.

Genesis 1:6

And God said, Let there be a firmament...let it divide...

Genesis 1:9

And God said, Let the waters under the heaven be gathered together into one place...and it was so.

Hebrews 11:3

Through faith we understand that the worlds were framed by the word of God, so that the things which are seen were not made of things which do appear.

b. God performs accomplishments of great significance on single days, or in short periods.

Genesis 1:9-13

On day three, God separated the earth and the seas, brought forth grasses, trees and all kinds of herbs.

c. God's creative acts have on occasion resulted in that which appears to be the end product of a continuing process.

Genesis 1:11

The grasses, herbs and trees were mature, yielding seed and fruit.

John 2:1-11

Likewise Christ produced wine at the wedding feast which normally would have required planting, growth, harvest and processing: yet it was superior to what they had had.

John 6:11-14

Here Jesus produced bread for the multitude without going through the normal process needed to make bread.

5. God preserves His creation so that it continues to function as He planned.

Genesis 1:11, 22, 28, 29, 30

God's plan for reproduction and for food.

Colossians 1:17

And he (Christ) is before all things, and by him all things consist (or hold together).

6. God controls every part of the natural world – His creation – the world we study in science.

This concept will be developed further in each section. A few illustrations are given here.

Job 9:5-7 (Job speaks of God)

5. He removes the mountains, and they do not know when He overturns them in His anger. 6. He shakes the earth out of its place, and its pillars tremble. 7. He commands the sun, and it does not rise, He seals off the stars.

Jonah 2:10

So the Lord spoke to the fish and it vomited Jonah onto dry land.

Jonah 4:6-8

6. And the Lord God prepared a plant and made it come up over Jonah... 7. God prepared a worm... 8...God prepared a vehement east wind ...

7. God created for His own purpose and pleasure.

Nehemiah 9:6

Thou, even thou, art Lord alone; thou

hast made heaven, the heavens...the host of heaven worshippeth thee.

I Corinthians 15:38 (Seeking of Sowing)
But God gives it a body as He pleased, and to each seed its own body.

Colossians 1:16
For by him all things were created...in heaven, and on earth...All things were created through Him and for Him.

Revelation 4:11 (A scene of worship in heaven)
...For You created all things, and by Your will they exist and were created.

10. God's creation was perfect in the beginning.

Genesis 1:4-12
4. And God saw the light, that it was good... 10. And God called the dry land Earth; and the gathering together of the waters called he Seas: and God saw that it was good. 12. And the earth brought forth grass...and the tree yielding fruit...and God saw that it was good, etc.

Genesis 1:27 (Man was God's image, and therefore was perfect)
So God created man in his own image, in the image God created he him; male and female created he them.

11. All of creation has been affected by man's sin.

Romans 5:12
Wherefore, as by one man sin entered into the world, and death by sin; and so death passed upon all men, for that all have sinned.

Romans 8:20-22

22. For we know that the whole creation groaneth and trevaileth with birth pangs together until now.

12. God has provided an orderly world.

Genesis 1:14 (At Creation)

And God said, Let there be lights...to divide the day from the night; and let them be for signs, and for seasons, and for days, and years.

Genesis 8:22 (After the Flood)

While the earth remaineth, seedtime and harvest, and cold and heat, and summer and winter and day and night shall not cease.

13. The natural world, God's creation, is constantly changing.

Job 14:19

As water wears away stones, and as torrents wash away the soil of the earth...

Isaiah 24:4 (Future)

The earth mourneth and fadeth away, the world languisheth and fadeth away...

Isaiah 40:7

The grass withereth, the flower fadeth...

Matthew 6:19

Lay not up for yourselves treasures upon earth, where moth and rust corrupt, and were thieves break through and steal.

14. God desires that we study science, the details of His Creation.

Genesis 1:28

...Be fruitful and multiply, and replenish the earth, and subdue it: and have dominion over the fish of the sea, and over the fowl of the air, and over every living thing that moveth upon the earth. (Subduing and having dominion implies studying and understanding.)

Job 12:7,8
7. But ask now the beasts, and they will teach you; and the birds of the air, and they will tell you: 8. Or speak to the earth, and it will teach you; and the fish of the sea will explain to you. As water wears away stones, and as torrents wash away the soil of the earth.

Matthew 6:26-30
26. Look at the birds of the air, for they neither sow nor reap nor gather into barns; yet your heavenly Father feeds them. Are you not of more value than they...

15. Man can never know all there is to know about the universe and about life.

Job 26:7-14
In verses 7-13 is a description of many acts of God related to the created world. Then follows: 14. Indeed these are the mere edges of His ways, and how small a whisper we hear of Him! But the thunder of His power who can understand?

Job 37
Most of this chapter tells of God's working which is beyond man's comprehension. Verse 5. God thunders marvelously with His voice; He does great things which we cannot comprehend.

Romans 11:33-34
33. O the depth of the riches both of the wisdom and knowledge of God! How unsearchable are

his judgments, and his ways past finding out! 34. For who hath known the mind of the Lord? Or who hath been his counselor?

16. Men by nature are not neutral or objective observers of God's universe; man's ability to understand the truth is impaired by sin.

Romans 1:18-32

19...Because what may be known of God is manifest in them; for God has shown it to them. 20. For since the creation of the world His invisible attributes are clearly seen, being understood by the things that are made, even His eternal power and Godhead, so that they are without excuse...

1 Corinthians 2:14

But the natural man does not receive the things of the Spirit of God, for they are foolishness to him; nor can he know them, they are spiritually discerned.

2 Peter 3:4-7 (Speaking of the scoffers in the last days)

4. And saying, Where is the promise of his coming? For since the fathers fell asleep, all things continue as they were from the beginning of creation. 5. For this they willingly are ignorant of, that by the word of God the heavens were of old, and the earth standing out of the water and in the water: 6. Whereby the world that then was, being overflowed with water, perished; 7. But the heavens and the earth, which are now, by the same word are kept in store, reserved unto fire against the day of judgment and perdition of ungodly men.

17. Seeming uniformity does not mean that God does not act in His universe. Refusal to accept this fact is willful ignorance. God everywhere condemns false teaching, and especially so when it undermines the faith of children.

Matthew 18:6

But whoso shall offend one of these little ones which believe in me, it were better for him that a millstone were hanged about his neck, and that he were drowned in the depth of the sea.

Psalm 1:1

Blessed is the man that walketh not in the counsel of the ungodly, nor standeth in the way of sinners, nor sitteth in the seat of the scornful.

Proverbs 19:27

Cease listening to instruction, my son, and you will stray from the words of knowledge.

Colossians 2:8

Beware lest any man spoil you through philosophy and van deceit, after the tradition of men, after the rudiments of the world, and not after Christ. (See also Hosea 4:6; and 2 Peter 2:1.)

There is much more that could be said about the statements of God's Bible. But the real issue is whether or not we accept the Word of God as truly our Creator's word. These were not total quotations from the Bible, but a combination of quotations and summary statements. I challenge you to see the need for a creation foundation, and I encourage you to watch the lives fall that build on any other foundations. The choice is simple – the solid rock foundation of God's Word, or the sand of man's wisdom. As for me, I'll take the rock.

William Cowper, 1731-1800, Doctor of Physics, Nobel Prize winner in physics, said in Missiles and Rockets, July 1957, "For myself, faith begins with a realization that a supreme intelligence brought the universe into being and created man. It is not difficult for me to have this faith, for it is incontrovertible that where there is a plan there is intelligence. An orderly, unfolding universe testifies to the truth of the most majestic statement ever uttered – 'In the beginning God.'"

"Nature is but a name for an effect whose cause is God."

V. GOD'S WORD: FOUNDATION FOR ALL CREATION

1. Do scientific evidences and scriptural statements coincide?

Yes, the findings of archeology, history, biology and the Bible are very harmonized. The problem is not that the evidence is not there. The problem is that man loves sin. Man does not want to be told that he is a sinner and that God will someday call him to stand and give an account of his life here on earth.

Man also knows that God hates sin. Man knows what sin is because of the Bible and his conscience. But man doesn't want to give up his sin. Therefore, he desires to find a way to reject God and still respect himself and be respected by others. The evolutionist's way is to discredit the Bible.

Atheism once was looked on as evil, sinful and blasphemous. But since the teaching of evolution, atheism has taken on a suit and tie. Professional people boldly say that they are atheists. Pride, arrogance, sinfulness, selfishness, etc., take over society. How many Salvation Army posts, food kitchens, hospitals and loving caring posts were started by the rejecters of God?

Yes, science and the Bible do go together! The good thing is that you do not need to take my word for it. I challenge you to look and see for yourselves if the Bible or evolution really tell the truth based on the evidence.

2. What are the fruits of the creation foundation?

The fruits of creation are love, joy, peace, etc. The fruit of creation teaching is a group of people with a purpose. The acceptance of God is to accept the creation of man in God's image with purpose and a reason to become your best.

The fruit of creation is good. Look back at the history of our own society. There was a time when we didn't even have to lock our doors because people knew that God had said, "Thou shalt not steal." There was a time when a life meant something, but now we have abortion, euthanasia, etc. Life is simply not valued.

3.   Conclusion

In conclusion, there have been battles among scientists, teachers, parents and now even religious leaders over evolution versus creation.

Every denomination has been affected by the evolution lie. For over one hundred years they have all battled the influence of the humanistic evolution foundation.

It is understandable for scientists and science teachers to battle over evolution. They have been taught the lies daily in their studies and many of them have no biblical foundation.

But God's men and women shouldn't struggle with the truth of our beginnings. Simply because the facts speak for themselves when they are examined. When the church struggles, that tells me when they are examined. When the church struggles, that tells me that we have done a very poor job educating our Christians as to the facts. That is why I have dedicated myself to writing this book as well as promoting other similar books that educate the church family. The truth will set you free!

Our church family needs to return to the foundations that gave them power—that being total reliance upon God and His Word as their sole authority. And they need to see that those foundations are powerfully true.

When the church and Christians struggle, what is the world to do? Remember, Jesus said, "Ye are the salt of the earth: but if the salt hath lost its savor, wherewith shall it be salted? It is thenceforth good for nothing, but to be cast out, and to be trodden underfoot of men" Matthew 5:13.

We are the salt, the decay stoppers. But if we lose our power, what hope is there for the rest of the world?

When even churches are having struggles within their ranks with the truth, is it any wonder that the rest of the world is in trouble and has swallowed the story of evolution? Especially the ones who are looking for a reason to reject God and His authority anyway. Our prayer is that *all* Christians will stay true to the foundation of God's Word. If we, as the church, leave the truth then we will inevitably have to accept the devastation and destruction this departure will bring.

The humanist teaching of evolution is not science but a system of beliefs (this becomes a religion). Think about that for a moment. The evolutionary theory doesn't hold water anyway. There isn't one bit of scientific proof for evolution. The evolutionists continue to talk with no substance. They are a religion without a revelation.

The evolutionist theory is like a disease that infects and destroys. Evolution leaves a trail of self-centered pain everywhere it is taught and accepted, whereas science glorifies God when a scientist studies present data and observes what is found from a premise of God as our Creator. Science's greatest hour was when God was God to the scientists.

In this study I have tried to examine evolution, its substance, its true humanistic root, and its devastation. I hope you have benefited from the study. I hope you will continue on in your studies and read others who share their insights into this very important topic. I also hope that you will share what you have learned and please do not keep it to yourself.

Although it is true that every problem in mankind is not a result of evolution, we must admit, every sin, every destructive force is a result of a no-God, self-centered mentality. Evolution, however, has become the spring board to publish sin into a more represented role in society. Now because of the wave of evolution we are suffering extreme problems.

Fruits of Evolution

1. It created doubts in all of God's Word.
2. It gave a foundation for attacking Christianity.

3. It caused marriages to become weak through selfishness.
4. It caused society to question the normal family structure.
5. It gave the atheists respectability.
6. It created a doubt in absolute truths.
7. It gave fuel for racism.
8. It promotes a lack of planning for tomorrow (a live for today mentality).
9. It took away the value of the human life (made in the image of God, now gone).
10. It established a respectable reason for rejecting God.

And many more ...

The damage is done, and devastation is upon us. Hosea 4:6-7 says, "My people are destroyed for lack of knowledge: because thou hast rejected knowledge, I will also reject thee, that thou shalt be no priest to me: seeing thou hast forgotten the law of thy God, I will also forget thy children. As they were increased, so they sinned against me: therefore will I change their glory into shame." Psalm 11:3 says, "If the foundations be destroyed, what can the righteous do?"

Proclaim the truth!

1. There is no truth to evolution.
2. Evolution has laid the foundation for many troubles we are now experiencing.
3. Science's greatest hour was founded upon God's Word.

4. The Bible and science are best friends when examined honestly.
5. We must inform others about all of these facts.

This is the first wave!

CHAPTER TWO

THE SECOND WAVE

ERODING THE CREATION FOUNDATION

If the foundations be destroyed,
what can the righteous do?
-- PSALM 11:3

I. THE REMOVAL OF HIS STORY

The disappearance of references to God in our history is a devastating tragedy that really took place as a result of the confusion over the statement of Thomas Jefferson when he referred to the need to separate the Church from the State. This statement is not in the Constitution of the United States but is in one of his letters. Jefferson never intended for his statement to be used to protect the State from the Church but to protect the Church from the State. Jefferson's statement in context with all of his other statements truly was in support of the teaching of Christianity to every child. To think otherwise is utterly foolish.

On January 1,1802, Jefferson wrote a letter to the Danbury Baptist Association of Danbury, Connecticut, calming their fears that Congress was not in the process of choosing any one single Christian denomination over another to be favored by government, as was the case with the Anglican Church in England and Virginia.

In his letter to the Danbury Baptists, who had experienced severe persecution for their faith, Jefferson borrowed phraseology from the famous Baptist minister Roger Williams who said, "...the hedge or wall of separation between the garden of the church and the wilderness of the world, God hath ever broken down the wall..." Jefferson's letter included:

> *Believing with you that religion is a matter which lies solely between man and his God, that he owes account to none other for faith actions only, and no opinions, I contemplate with solemn reverence that act of the whole American people which declared that their legislature should "make no law respecting an establishment of religion, or prohibiting the free exercise thereof," thus building a wall of separation between Church and State.*[vii]

This personal letter reassured the Baptists that the government's hands were tied from interfering with, or in any way controlling, the affairs or decisions of the church in America. The Association of Baptists was concerned that the State was going to start favoring one denomination over another. Jefferson was responding to their fears. He was *not* saying that the state should not promote the Bible or the Christian faith. In his day Christianity was the only religion in America to be considered. If you were not a Christian you were an atheist. Jefferson knew that Christianity was a powerful driving force in the Colonies. By other statements of Jefferson we can see his extreme appreciation of it.

Thomas Jefferson did not sign the Constitution, nor was he present at the Constitutional Convention of 1787. Neither was he present when the First Amendment and religious freedom was debated in the first session of Congress in 1789, as he was out of the country in France as a U.S. Minister. Due to his not being present to hear all the comments of the Founding Fathers regarding the First Amendment, Jefferson had to rely on secondhand information to learn what had transpired in that first session of Congress. This rendered his letter to the Danbury Baptists (which was written 13 years after the first Amendment) ineligible to be considered a "firsthand" reflection of the intent of the constitutional delegates.

It is amazing how a people will believe anything if it's repeated enough. Our forefathers were very dedicated to teaching Christianity and the values of Christianity to the future generations of America. They knew that without morality and virtue this country could not stand.

Who among us has not heard of the Separation of Church and State? Who among us realizes that this separation of Church and State statement is *not* in the Constitution, nor is it a part of the First Amendment?

The First Amendment: Congress shall make no law respecting an establishment of religion or prohibiting the free exercise thereof; or abridging the freedom of speech or of the press; or the right of the people peaceably to assemble, and to petition the government for a redress of grievances.

This statement made by Jefferson has been drawn like a gun challenging anyone who wanted to name the name of Christ on school grounds. And now even in government offices the statement is being used to keep government employees from sharing their faith and or even enjoying their Christian faith on the job. They are simply told to leave their religion at home! The government is not to promote religion! When in *truth* the statement was not a law nor was it to stop the promoting of religion. It was made to assure the religious people that the state would not favor one Christian denomination over another.

Our leaders believed in favoring Christianity over every other religion and there is no questioning that if we only read what they wrote.

On October 11, 1798, President John Adams stated in his address to the military:

> *We have no government armed with power capable of contending with human passions unbridled by morality and religion. Avarice, ambition, revenge, or gallantry, would break the strongest cords of*

our Constitution as a whale goes through a net. Our Constitution was made only for a moral and religious people. It is wholly inadequate to the government of any other.[viii]

Our Founding Fathers' lives and attitude toward the Church and its teachings display very strong beliefs that our country needs the Bible and its teachings. We will discuss this further in the section on the Founding Fathers.

From 1920 and up as evolution was being taught to the children as the first wave of destruction, the leaders knew that they were teaching two different stories. They were teaching in the science class that we came from nothing. But in history class they were teaching that our forefathers, our discoverers, our purposes and our hopes were in our Creator. This was a confusion to our children without a doubt. The educators' answer then was to remove God from the history class just as they were removing God from the science class. This was the beginning of the second wave as people are continually carried along until the third wave—watering down the word.

I hope you will understand the conspiracy by the humanist's to remove God from America and in turn replace Him with a god of man worship. This in turn is leading to a devastation to our great country. Let me explain.

The first thing that the humanists had to do was to replace the word for history with the words Social Study.

Noah Webster's definitions:

History - *History and Story are the same word differently written. A Story with the prefix His in front. His story or History.*

Social - *From the Latin word socius, companion. Pertaining to society: relating to men living in society, or to the public as an aggregate body; as social interests or concerns; social pleasures; social benefits; social happiness; social duties. Ready or disposed to mix in friendly converse; companionable. Social is referring to man in his relationship with others.*

Studies - *To apply the mind to; to read and examine for the purpose of learning and understanding.*

Social
Studies - *To learn how people relate to people.*

The word for history is without question a direct statement referring to a Creator, (His Story). Their plan has been to erase the mention of God from the ears of our students in the class rooms and turn remove God from future generations.   As Abraham Lincoln said, the attitudes of the class room today will be the attitudes of society tomorrow.   The war of the future is won or lost in the class room.   We are losing that war.   The word history was replaced with the words social study.   Most of us do not even know how or when the change took place, but it did take place. Let me mention a few other word changes that society is missing and didn't even notice.   Christmas break in our schools was replaced with Winter break.   Easter break was replaced with Spring break. You see, it's a war of words.   Communication, education and formation of a society are waged as a war of words.   The humanist knows this, but we are slow to catch on. Most of our America didn't even realize we were under attack until very special jewels came up missing from society, jewels like virtue, purity, morality, honesty, kindness, compassion, love, conscience, etc.   These were jewels given to America through a knowledge of the Bible and a relationship with Jesus Christ.   Without this knowledge or relationship, these jewels will disappear forever. You and I must understand that we are in a war for our future. A no God society leads to death. We must fight to keep God, Christ, and the Bible in our language and in our lives.

These terms: history, Social Studies, Christmas, Easter break, etc., began to be missing as this misunderstanding over the Separation of Church and State issue became distorted.   One event in American history that gave them a tremendous boost in their plight to remove God and enhance the confusion of the Separate of Church and State issue was the decision to remove prayer from the classroom in 1963. We in America were already staggering as a result of 50 years of evolutionary teaching. Fifty years is at least 4 total school-educated groups from the first grade to the twelfth.

The Scopes trial in Dayton, Tennessee in 1925 established an open door for the evolutionists to proclaim their destructive lie. Then in 1963 another rocket was launched by the rejecters of God in their effort to remove God from before the face of our students and society.

In 1963, an atheistic woman walked her son into a public school in Baltimore, Maryland to enroll him in their program of education. The woman was Madalyn Murray O'Hair, a member of the communist party who had tried to become a Russian citizen, but was refused by the Russian leaders. As she walked down the hall to the office, she heard the praying of a teacher in a classroom. As she enrolled her child, she told the principal she didn't want her son exposed to this religious teaching, and demanded that they stop praying in the school and stop teaching religion. The principal refused, and the school was dragged into a law suit that later became the devastating decision that told the school they could not initiate prayer nor teach religion in a government school.

According to Bill Murray, O'Hair's son, she became an instantly wealthy woman. Before the suit they were living on government assistance, but they began to receive large checks in the mail. These checks were from wealthy rejecters of God.

O'Hair was not an instant hero to the humanistic teachers and atheistic promoters everywhere.

If you would like more information on this subject, write William J. Murray Evangelism Association, P.O. Box 2200, Stafford, Virginia 22555, or call (540) 659-0386. Mr. Murray has since received Jesus as Savior, and is now telling the truth behind the dilemma of 1963. Bill has written several books, and is a man with a story that began in sadness, but became victorious when he received the God his mother had worked so hard to reject. His mother has since disappeared without a trace, and no one seems to know where she is.

No one really conceived the future growth of this 1963 ruling that acted as a seed. To the humanist, this meant no prayer, no Bible, no religious clothing, no religious talking on government property. You see, to the man who was trying to erase God from before the face of America's students and society, this was the ammunition he had been looking for.

As the removal took place, motivated first by the Scope's trial and evolution teaching, then by O'Hair's law suit, His Story (History) then was changed to Studies of Social Behaviors. Progressively, the students began more and more to look to the world for answers and not to the God of our country.

The God of our country—a statement that in 1998 is hard to imagine being once so well accepted as fact. But it is true, we were and still are a country formed by God. Our early leaders really believed this. Let me illustrate this in the coming pages.

II. The foundation of American wisdom and Truth (Our Forefathers' Statements)

Our forefathers were living their lives with the belief that God (the Father of Jesus Christ) was the Creator of the universe. They believed that He was involved in the lives of men. The believed that they were here to be God's instruments in His providential handiwork. *Providential – Provider God, the hand of God providing.*

The belief in God's Providence is why the forefathers said these great words of belief. Let's begin with the Continental Congress, in its beginning:

Continental Congress June 28, 1787, Thursday, found the Constitutional Convention embroiled in a bitter debate over how each state was to be represented in the new government. The hostile feelings created by the smaller states being pitted against the larger states, was so bitter that some delegates actually left the Convention.

Benjamin Franklin, being the President (Governor) of Pennsylvania, hosted the rest of the 55 delegates attending the Convention. Being senior member of the convention, at 81 years of age, he commanded the respect of all present, and as recorded in James Madison's detailed records, he arose to address the Congress in this moment of crisis:

Mr. President, the small progress we have made after four or five weeks' close attendance and continual reasoning with each other-our different sentiments on almost every question, several of the last producing as many noes as ayes, is methinks a melancholy proof of the imperfection of the Human Understanding.

We indeed seem to feel our own want of political wisdom, since we have been running about in search of it. We have gone back to ancient history for models of government, and examined the different forms of those Republics, which, having been formed with the seeds of their own dissolution, now no longer exist. And we have viewed Modern States all around Europe, but find none of their Constitutions suitable to our circumstances.

In the situation of this Assembly, groping as it were in the dark to find political truth, and scarce able to distinguish it when presented to us, how has it happened, Sir, that we have not hitherto once thought of humbly applying to the

Father of Lights to illuminate our understanding?

In the beginning of this Contest with Great Britain, when we were sensible of danger we had daily prayer in this room for the Divine protection—Our prayers, Sir, were heard, and they were graciously answered.   All of us who were engaged in the struggle must have observed frequent instances of a superintending providence in our favor.

To that kind providence we owe this happy opportunity of consulting in peace on the means of establishing our future national felicity. And have we now forgotten that powerful Friend?   Or do we imagine we no longer need His assistance?

I have lived, Sir, a long time and the longer I live, the more convincing proofs I see of this truth – that God Governs in the affairs of men, and if a sparrow cannot fall to the ground without His notice, is it probable that an empire can rise without his aid?

We have been assured, Sir, in the Sacred Writings, that "except the Lord build the House, they labor in vain that build it."   I firmly believe this; and I also believe this; and I also believe that without his concurring aid we shall succeed in this political building no better than the builder of Babel: We shall be divided by our partial local interests; our projects will be confounded, and we ourselves shalt become a reproach and by word down to future ages. And what is worse, mankind may hereafter from this unfortunate instance, despair of establishing Governments by Human wisdom and leave in to chance, war and conquest.

I therefore beg leave to move-- that henceforth prayers imploring the assistance of Heaven, and its blessing on our deliberations, be held in this Assembly every morning before we proceed to business, and that one or more of the clergy of this city be requested to officiate in that service.[ix]

We hear very little said about the statement made by Mr. Franklin, frankly because of his continual references to God and our need for Him.

Continental Congress July 8, 1776, for the first time read the Declaration of Independence publicly, as the famous "Liberty Bell" was rung. Congress then established a three-man committee, consisting of Thomas Jefferson, John Adams and Benjamin Franklin, for the purpose of designing a great seal for the United States.

Benjamin Franklin's suggestions for a seal and motto, characterizing the spirit of this new nation, were:

Moses lifting up his wand, and dividing the Red Sea, and pharaoh in his chariot overwhelmed with the waters. This motto: "Rebellion to tyrants is obedience to God."

Thomas Jefferson proposed:

The children of Israel in the wilderness, led by a cloud by day, and a pillar of fire by night.[x]

These two men are said to have been the two least religious of the three, but in these statements you would thing they were the most religious of the nation. There is no doubt by their statements, these men knew that the God of the Bible was the power behind the founding of America.

Question: have you ever heard of these proposals by these men? If so, I dare say you are an exception.

Continental Congress July 9, 1776, on the day following the first public reading of the Declaration of Independence in Philadelphia and the ringing of the "Liberty Bell" moved to establish prayer as a daily part of this new nation:

Resolved, That the Rev. Mr. J. Duche' be appointed chaplain to

Congress, and that he be desired *to attend every morning at 9 o'clock.*[xi]

Let me encourage you to think a minute. Do you think the Founding Fathers would have wanted to start their day in prayer but stop their children from starting the day with prayer? Do you think they would want God's help in the halls of the day with prayer? Do you think they would want God's help in the halls of Congress but refuse the children from calling on the Creator in the classrooms? I don't think so!

Continental Congress July 9, 1776, authorized the Continental Army to provide chaplains for their troops. On the same day, General George Washington, the Commander-in-Chief of the Continental Army, issued the order to appoint chaplains to every regiment. In his first general order to his troops, General George Washington called on:

Every officer and man...to live, and act, as becomes a Christian Soldier defending the dearest Rights and Liberties of his country.[xii]

Continental Congress September 11, 1777, approved and recommended to the people that 20,000 copies of the Holy Bible be imported from other sources. This was in response to the shortages of Bibles in America caused by the Revolutionary War interrupting trade with England. The Chaplain of Congress, Patrick Allison, brought the matter to the attention of

Congress, who assigned it to a special Congressional Committee, which reported:

The use of the Bible is so universal and its importance so great that your committee refers the above to the consideration of Congress, and if Congress shall not think it expedient to order the importation of types and paper, the Committee recommends that Congress will order the Committee of Commerce to import 20,000 Bibles from Holland, Scotland, or elsewhere, into the different parts of the States of the Union.

Whereupon it was resolved accordingly to direct said Committee of Commerce to import 20,000 copies of the Bible.[xiii]

Continental Congress July 13, 1787, passed "An Ordinance for the Government of the Territory of the United States, North-West of the River Ohio," later shortened to the Northwest ordinance. (This ordinance was later passed by the United States Congress, and signed into law by President George Washington, August 4, 1789, just as the First Amendment was being formulated):

Article3 III Religion, morality, and knowledge being necessary to good government and the happiness of mankind, schools and the means of education shall be forever encouraged.[xiv]

Notice—Religion, morality, government, schools, and education all together!

These are only a few of the examples that could have been cited. I think you can see the consistency of these men and their faith in God. I hope you can see their deep dependence upon the God of the Bible, their gratitude, their dedication, and their belief in its importance and power. Can you imagine these men banning the Bible from government schools?

What about their personal statements? Let's discuss just a few:

Thomas Jefferson

Thomas Jefferson (1743-1826), an author, architect, educator and scientist, was the third President of the United States of America. In 1774, while serving in the Virginia Assembly, he personally introduced a resolution calling for a Day of Fasting and Prayer.

Thomas Jefferson penned the words of the Declaration of Independence on July 4, 1776:

> *When in the Course of human events, it becomes necessary for one people to dissolve the political bands which have connected them with another, and to assume among the powers of the earth, the separate and*

equal station to which the Laws of Nature and of Nature's God entitles them...

We hold these truths to be self-evident, that all men are created equal. That they are endowed by their Creator with certain inalienable rights, that among these are life...

We, therefore, the Representatives of the United States of America, in General Congress, Assembled, appealing to the Supreme Judge of the world for the rectitude of our intentions...

And for the support of this Declaration, with a firm reliance on the protection of divine Providence, we mutually pledge to each other our Lives, our Fortunes and our sacred Honor.

In 1781, Jefferson made these statements in Query XVIII of his Notes on the State of Virginia. Excerpts of these statements are engraved on the Jefferson Memorial in Washington, D.C.:

God who gave us life gave us liberty. And can the liberties of a nation by thought secure when we have removed their only firm basis, a conviction in the minds of the people that these liberties are of the Gift of God? That they are not to be violated

buy with His wrath?   Indeed, I
tremble for my country when I reflect
that God is just; that His justice
cannot sleep forever.[xv]

Thomas Jefferson, while being the third President (1801-1809), chaired the school board for the District of Columbia, where he authored the first plan of education adopted by the city of Washington, which used the Bible and Isaac Watts' Hymnal as the principal books to teach reading to students.

On March 23, 1801, Thomas Jefferson wrote from Washington, D.C. to Moses Robinson:

The Christian Religion, when
divested of the rages in which they
(the clergy) have enveloped it, and
brought to the original purity and
simplicity of its benevolent institutor,
is a religion of all others most
friendly to liberty, science, and the
freest expansion of the human mind.[xvi]

Now remember, Jefferson is the man that the courts in 1963 said was against teaching religion in the schools. Their total basis for no prayer or Bible teaching in the government school was Jefferson's statement of Separation of Church and State. They teach that Jefferson was against the government schools teaching the Bible when, in truth, he was the one who promoted the Bible and the Bible Hymns in the class and schools of our United States.

John Adams

John Adams (1735-1826), was the second President of the United States of America and the first President to live in the White House. He had also served as the Vice-President for eight years under President George Washington. The Library of Congress and the Department of the Navy were established under his presidency.

A graduate of Harvard, John Adams became a member of the Continental Congress and a signer of the Declaration of Independence. He is distinguished for having personally urged Thomas Jefferson to write the Declaration, as well as for having recommended George Washington as the Commander-in-Chief of the Continental Army. He was the main author of the Constitution of Massachusetts in 1780. John Adams was the U.S. Minister to France, and, along with John Jay and Benjamin Franklin, helped negotiate the treaty with Great Britain ending the Revolutionary War. Later he was U.S. Minister to Britain. During this time, he greatly influenced the American states to ratify the Constitution by writing a three-volume work entitled, *A Defense of the Constitution of the Government of the United States.*

In his diary entry dated February 22, 1756, John Adams wrote:

> *Suppose a nation is some distant region should take the Bible for their only book, and every member should regulate his conduct by the precepts there exhibited! Every member would*

be obliged in conscience, to temperance, frugality, and industry; to justice, kindness, and charity towards his fellow men; and to piety, love, and reverence toward Almighty God...What a Eutopia, what a Paradise would this region be.[xvii]

On June 21, 1776, Adam wrote:

Statesmen, my dear Sir, may plan and speculate for liberty, but it is **Religion and Morality alone, which can establish the Principles upon which Freedom can securely stand.**

The only foundation of a free Constitution is pure virtue, and if this cannot be inspired into our people in a greater measure than they have it now, they may change their rulers and the forms of government, but they will not obtain a lasting liberty [bold added].

In contemplating the effect that separation from England would mean to him personally, John Adams wrote:

If it be the pleasure of Heaven that my country shall require the poor offering of my life, the victim shall be ready, at the appointed hour of sacrifice, come when they hour may.

But while I do live, let me have a country, and that a free country.[xviii]

On July 1, 1776, John Adams profoundly spoke at the Continental Congress to the delegates from the Thirteen Colonies:

Before God, I believe the hour has come. My judgment approves this measure, and my whole heart is in it. All that I have, and all that I am, and all that I hope in this life, I am now ready here to stake upon it. And I leave off as I began, that live or die, survive or perish, I am for the Declaration. It is my living sentiment, and by the blessing of God it shall be my dying sentiment, Independence now, and Independence forever![xix]

On June 2, 1778, John Adams made this journal entry in Paris:

In vain are Schools, Academies, and Universities institutioned, if loose Principles and licentious habits are impressed upon Children in their earliest years... The Vices and Examples of the Parents cannot be concealed from the Children. How is it possible that Children can have any just Sense of the sacred Obligations of Morality or Religion if, from their earliest Infancy, they learn their Mothers live in habitual Infidelity to their fathers, and their fathers in as constant Infidelity to their Mothers?

In a letter to Thomas Jefferson, John Adams wrote:

> *Have you ever found in history one single example of a Nation thoroughly corrupted that was afterwards restored to virtue?... And without virtue, there can be no political liberty...Will you tell me how to prevent riches from becoming the effects of temperance and industry? Will you tell me how to prevent luxury from producing effeminacy, intoxication, extravagance, vice and folly? I believe no effort favor of virtue is lost...*

In a letter to Thomas Jefferson, December 25, 1813, John Adams wrote:

> *I have examined all religions, as well as my narrow sphere, my straightened means, and busy life, would allow; and the result is that the Bible is the best book in the world. It contains more philosophy than all the libraries I have seen.*[xx]

On April 19, 1817, John Adams wrote in a letter to Thomas Jefferson:

Without religion, this world would be something not fit to be mentioned in polite company.

...The most abandoned scoundrel that ever existed, never yet wholly extinguished his Conscience and while Conscience remains, there is some religion.[xxi]

George Washington

George Washington (1732-1799), the first President of the United States, was the Commander-in-Chief of the Continental Army during the Revolutionary War. He was also a surveyor, a planter and a soldier, as well as a statesman. In addition to being politically involved as the chairman of the Constitutional Convention, George Washington was also an active Episcopalian. Considered the most popular man in the Colonies, George Washington was described by Henry "Light Horse Harry" Lee in his now famous tribute, as "First in war, first in peace, first in the hearts of his countrymen."

The son of Augustine Washington and his second wife, Mary Ball, George Washington was also a descendent of King John of England, as well as one of the twenty-five Baron Sureties of the Magna Carta. His father died when he was eleven years old in 1743, and from then until the age of sixteen, George lived with his elder half-brother, Augustine, in Westmoreland County, Virginia, just 40 miles outside of Fredericksburg. Most of George's education was through home schooling and tutoring. He received his surveyor's license in 1749 from William and Mary College and later, from 1788 until death, was the college's chancellor.

At age 15, George Washington copied, in his own handwriting, *110 Rules of Civility and Decent Behavior in Company and Conversation.* Among them were:

> *When you speak of God, or His attributes, let it be seriously and with reverence. Honor and obey your natural parents although they be poor.*

> *Let your recreations be manful not sinful.*

> *Labor to keep alive in your breast that little spark of celestial fire called conscience.*

When George Washington was leaving home to begin what would become a lifelong service for his country, he recorded the parting words of his mother, Mrs. Mary Washington:

> *Remember that is our only sure trust. To Him, I commend you... My son, neglect not the duty of secret prayer.*

The account of George Washington at the Battle at the Monongahela was included in students' textbooks in America until 1934. During the French and Indian War, George Washington fought alongside of the British General Edward Braddock. On July 9, 1755, the British were on the way to Fort Duquesne, when the French surprised them in an ambush attack.

The British, who were not accustomed to fighting unless in an open field, were being annihilated. Washington rode back and forth across the battle delivering General Braddock's orders. As the battle raged, every other officer on horseback, except Washington, was shot down, until even General Braddock was killed, at which point the troops fled in confusion. After the babble, on July 18, 1755, Washington wrote to his brother, John A. Washington:

> *But by the all-powerful dispensations of Providence, I have been protected beyond all human probability or expectation; for I had four bullets through my coat, and two horses shot under me, yet escaped unhurt, although death was leveling my companions on every side of me!*

Fifteen years later, Washington and Dr. Craik, a close friend of his from his youth, were traveling through those same woods near the Ohio River and Great Kanawha River. They were met by an old Indian chief, who addressed Washington through an interpreter:

> *I am a chief and ruler over my tribes. My influence extends to the*

waters of the great lakes and to the far blue mountains.

I have traveled a long and weary path that I might see the young warrior of the great battle. It was on the day when the white man's blood mixed with the streams of our forest that I beheld this chief (Washington).

I called to my young men and said, mark yon tall and daring warrior. He is not of the red-coat tribe—he hath an Indian's wisdom, and his warriors fight as we do— himself alone exposed.

Quick, let your aim be certain, and he dies. Our rifles were leveled, rifles which, but for you, knew not how to miss—'twas all in vain. A power mightier far than we, shielded you.

Seeing you were under the special guardship of the Great Spirit, we immediately ceased to fire at you. I am old and soon shall be gathered to the council fire of my fathers in the land of shades, but ere I go, there is something bids me speak in the voice of prophecy:

Listen! The Great Spirit protects that man (pointing to Washington), and guides his *destinies—he will become the chief of nations, and a people yet unborn will hail him as the founder of a mighty empire. I am come to pay homage to the man who is the particular favorite of Heaven, and who can never die in battle.*

The famous Indian warrior, who was in the battle, said:

Washington was never born to be killed by a bullet! I had seventeen fair fires at him with my rifle, and after all could not bring him to the ground![xxii]

These are the historical facts that once were a part of the history books. Notice the Social Study books of today. Try to find anything close to this story today. I dare say if you are not older than fifty years or very involved in some special personal study, you have never heard any of these statements about Washington. These are the kinds of changes about which I am trying to alert our nation.

On June 1, 1774, as the Colonies were seeking God's will as to whether they should break ties with England, George Washington made this entry in his diary.

Went to church and fasted all day.[xxiii]

On July 4, 1775, in his General Orders from Headquarters at Cambridge, General George Washington gave the order:

The General most earnestly requires and expects a due observance of those articles of war established for the government of the Army which forbid profane cursing, swearing and drunkenness. And in like manner he requires and expects of all officers and soldiers not engaged in actual duty, a punctual attendance of Divine services, to implore the blessing of Heaven upon the means used for our safety and defense. [xxiv]

The Navy cruisers commissioned by General Washington during the Revolutionary War flew as their ensign a white flag with a green pine tree and above it the inscription:

An Appeal to Heaven [xxv]

On July 9, 1776, the Continental Congress authorized the Continental Army to provide chaplains for their troops. General Washington then issued the order and appointed chaplains to every regiment. In that same day, he issued the general order to his troops, stating:

The General hopes and trusts that every officer and man will endeavor so the live, and act, as becomes a Christian Soldier defending the dearest Rights and Liberties of his country.[xxvi]

General George Washington's prayer:

And now, Almighty Father, if it be Thy holy will that we shall obtain a place and name among the nations of the earth, grant that we may be enabled to show our gratitude for Thy goodness by our endeavors to fear and obey Thee. Bless us with wisdom in our counsels, success in battle, and let all our victories be tempered with humanity. Endow, also, our enemies with enlightened minds, that they become sensible of their injustice, and willing to restore our liberty and peace. Grant the petition of Thy servant, for the sake of Him whom Thou hast called Thy believe Son; nevertheless, not my will, but Thine be done.[xxvii]

There's much, much more that could be said about George Washington the soldier, the General, the President, the Christian. But I feel you understand the kind of man God gave us for the Father of our Country, as he is called. The shame of it is that our new generations will never know these very special things about this man; such a shame.

This is just one very enlightening example of the thieves who have slipped into America and have stolen our children's Christian heritage.

Henry Clay

Henry Clay (1777-1852), was a powerful U.S. Senator who also served as a Congressman. He was elected Speaker of the House six times, and for nearly 40 years was a leading American statesman. Clay was part of the "Great Triumvirate" with Daniel Webster and John Calhoun, which dominated Congress during the early to mid-1800s. Known as the Great Compromiser, Clay was able to keep the North and the South together as the Union for many years. Although he was a Presidential candidate several times, Clay never was elected.

In 1839, when he was about to give a speech in which he would declare himself against slavery, one of his friends warned him that this would ruin his chances to become President. To this, Henry Clay gave his famous reply:

> *I would rather be right than President.*[xxviii]

From a speech to the Kentucky Colonization Society, at Frankfort, 1829, Henry Clay proclaimed:

> *Eighteen hundred years have rolled away since the Son of God, our blessed Redeemer, offered Himself on Mount Calvary for the salvation of our species; and more than half of mankind still continue to deny His Divine mission and the truth of His sacred Word...*

*When we shall, as soon we
must, be translated from this into
another form of existence, it is the
hope presumptuous that we shall
behold the common Father of the
whites and blacks, the great Ruler of
the Universe, case his all-seeing eye
upon civilized and regenerated
Africa, its cultivated fields, its coasts
stubbed with numerous cities,
adorned with towering temples
dedicated to the pure religion of his
redeeming son?*[xxix]

Henry Clay confided with Congress
Venerable:

*I am not afraid to die, sir; I
hope faith, and some confidence; I
have an abiding trust in the merits
and meditation of our Saviour.*[xxx]

John Jay

John Jay (1745-1829), was the first Chief
Justice of the United States Supreme Court,
having been appointed by President George
Washington. He was a Foundation Father, and a
member of the First and Second Continental
Congress. He was very instrumental in causing
the Constitution to be ratified by writing the
Federalist Papers, along with James Madison and
Alexander Hamilton. In 1777, John Jay helped to
write the Constitution of New York, and from

1795-1801 held the position of Governor of the State of New York.

> *John Jay negotiated the peace treaty to end the War with England (along with John Adams and Benjamin Franklin). He was Secretary of Foreign Affairs under the Articles of Confederation, minister to Spain and in 1794 he authored the Jay Treaty which prevented the United States from getting involved in the war between France and England.*[xxxi]

On October 12, 1816, John Jay admonished:

> *Providence has given to our people the choice of their rulers, and it is the duty, as well as the privilege and interest of our Christian nation to select and prefer Christians for their rulers.*[xxxii]

In addition to being appointed by President George Washington as the first Chief Justice of the United States Supreme Court, John Jay was also elected president of the Westminster Bible Society in 1818 and president of the American Bible Society in 1821.

On May 13, 1824, serving as its president, John Jay gave an address to the American Bible Society:

By conveying the Bible to people thus circumstanced, we certainly do them a most interesting kindness. We thereby enable them to learn that man was originally created and placed in a state of happiness, but, becoming disobedient, was subjected to the degradation and evils which he and his posterity have since experienced.

The Bible will also inform them that our gracious Creator provided for us a Redeemer, in whom all the nations of the earth shall be blessed; that this Redeemer has made atonement "for the sins of the whole world," and thereby reconciling the Divine justice with the Divine mercy has opened a way for our redemption and salvation; and that these inestimable benefits are of the free gift and grace of God, not of our deserving, nor in our power to deserve.[xxxiii]

John Hancock

John Hancock (1737-1793), an American merchant and Revolutionary leader, was the president of the Provincial Congress of Massachusetts. He became well-known for having been the first member of the Constitutional Congress to sign the Declaration of Independence.

On April 15, 1775, the Provincial Congress of Massachusetts declared A Day of Public Humiliation, Fasting and Prayer, signed by the President of the Provincial Congress, John Hancock:

In circumstances dark as these, it becomes us, as Men and Christians, to reflect that, whilst every prudent Measure should be taken to ward off the impending Judgements...All confidence must be withheld from the Means we use; and respond only on the God who rules in the Armies of Heaven, and without whose Blessing the best human Counsels are but Foolishness—and all created Power Vanity;

It is the Happiness of his Church that, when the Powers of Earth and Hell combine against it...that the Throne of Grace is of the easiest access—and its Appeal hither is graciously invited by the Father of Mercies, who has assured it, that when his Children ask Bread he will not give them a Stone...

Resolved, That it be, and hereby is recommended to the good People of this Colony of all Denominations, that Thursday the Eleventh Day of May next be set apart as a Day of Public Humiliation, Fasting and Prayer...to confess the sins...to implore the Forgiveness of all our Transgression...and a blessing on the Husbandry, Manufactures, and other lawful Employments of this People; and especially that the union of the American Colonies in Defense of their Rights (for hitherto we desire to thank Almighty God) may be preserved and confirmed...And that America may soon behold a gracious Interposition of Heaven.

By Order of the (Massachusetts) Provincial Congress, John Hancock, President. [xxxiv]

Other Great Men

Alexander Hamilton (signer of the Constitution, author of 51 of the 85 Federalist Papers, and captain of a New York artillery unit in the Revolutionary Way) John Harvard, Patrick Henry, etc.

The Founding Fathers were, without question, men who understood the importance of God's Word to morality, and the importance of morality to the future of a nation.

Therefore, this separation of Church and State decision of 1963 that the ACLU continues to use to threaten those who try to give conscience and morality to our nation, is without question a big mistake, and a disaster.

Let's examine and compare true History to the Social Studies taught today.

III. ARE HISTORY AND SOCIAL STUDIES THE SAME?

10 Stages of Providential History and The Teachings of Social Studies Compared

In this section I will give you an idea of the true 10 stages of history that our Founding Fathers knew. I would like to give you a little taste of the history our Founding Fathers were taught.

When you hear and understand what they had been taught, you will understand why they were the men they were. Our Founding Fathers were full of wisdom, and willingness to sacrifice all they had for the cause of liberty. On occasion, history might paint the picture of one individual who rises above others in their abilities and actions. But at the time of America's founding, there were hundreds and even thousands who were above the world in wisdom and a willingness to sacrifice.

The world is still talking about the amazing people of our founding. When history is examined at the Founding Fathers' time, we find one very powerful fact. The Bible was the central text book in every subject. The Bible was accepted as the authority without question by most of the Founding Fathers. Their own statements testify to this. I know there are people who try to say that some of these men were not believers or what we would call devoted Christians. I am not saying that all of these were devoted totally to the cause of Christ. But some of them were.

Also, let me say, even the ones who were not totally devoted to Christ respected Him and did not argue with the authority or power of the Word of God. At the time of the founding of America, it is well said that 98% were believers in the authority of the Bible. That is why any statements the men made to promote Bibles or prayer meetings were never met with opposition.

Question: Why were so many people full of wisdom, convictions, and godly character at that time?

Answer: Because of the Great Awakening that had taken place just a few years before this time in England and had spilled over into the colonies.

Because of the struggles in England over spiritual matters the Pilgrims came to the New World. But after their departure God sent a great revival to England, a revival of preaching of the Word of God. This Revival spilled over into America. The Colonies in turn experienced a great revival called by historians, "The Great Awakening." This revival had many preachers, but the one that stands out the most is George Whitefield. Whitefield preached all up and down the eastern seaboard with power. Whitefield was respected by all the Founding Fathers who I dare say were affected by his preaching in extreme ways. Benjamin Franklin has a lot to say about the great power of George Whitefield.

These men were tutored by their mothers or special tutors. The Bible was the center of every subject. Science, Math, English, History, etc., was looked at and taught through the eyes of the Bible. Therefore, Jesus was their hero and example. God was the Creator. Man was the instrument that God used to get His will performed. God was their protector and provider, and was very much involved in their everyday lives and decision making (Providence.)

When we know how they were taught, we understand why they said the things they said and did the things they did. But most of all we realize why they had the wisdom, attitudes, sacrificial will, bravery, etc., that they possessed.

When I compare History to Social Studies, I am telling the story of History from a Bible-based premise. I am telling History the way our Founding Fathers were taught History. When I am telling the Social Study Story, I am telling the past from a strictly no God premise, simply people interacting with people based on their own need for power and survival. Really, this is from an evolutionary foundation.

You really do not need to take my word for this. Simply collect history books from our early history and the events are told. The stories are sometimes so differently told that we often would wonder if they are talking about the same place and time.

Let's walk through a History, Social Studies comparison.

1. We must start with Creation

History —

Our old history writers and Founding Fathers believed that we were endowed by our Creator. They made many, many statements that showed they believed in creation. They believed in the Creator because of their acceptance of the Bible. Creation comes from the Bible, and the Bible was the central text book to all education. Therefore, they believed we were created. Adam and Eve were the first people created by God.

a. The creation of all things including man. We have a responsibility to the Creator. Man has a driving force in him that wants to do right.

b. The fall of man. This is the story that explains to man why they have a driving force in them that wants to do wrong. This also tells them that they need some help to overcome this sin that lives inside of them. The Bible teaches us that man was created and then tested. The testing was in short whether or not the man would believe God's Word or another influence, namely the serpent or devil in disguise. Eve believed the serpent, and therefore Adam also followed her lead, probably to keep her and not be separated from her.

Therefore, the fall of man is a major tragedy that destroys and sets the state for man's sin dilemma.

This creation teaching answers the many questions that we face every day. Such as, why do people die? Why do men and women marry and raise a family? Who is responsible to take care of the family? Why do we wear clothing, etc.?

History from a Bible perspective teaches that we will stand before God and give an account for our lives and especially our response to the person of Jesus Christ. Since we will stand before God and give an account, we need to live a life that will be pleasing to us in the Day of Judgment and not only us but to the Creator to whom we will be responsible.

Social Studies--

The secular Social Studies approach answers all the questions of creation from an evolutionary approach. They believe that man came from a mud pit and essentially created himself. WE die because of the natural laws of the stronger squeezing out the weaker. The reason we marry is because of the teaching of religious people who developed the customs that we live by today. They believe we have no one that we are responsible to, so therefore, we are our own boss. We have no afterlife to look forward to, nor a

Creator to give an account to, Therefore, eat, drink and be merry, because soon we die.

2. Moses and the Law

History –

Moses and the law came in a time of Jewish history that was important to the formation of the Jewish state. But our early historians believed that the history of the Jews and the history of the world were inseparable. The Jewish God was the God of the world and Creator of America. He was the Creator of all. Therefore, we have the laws God gave them, and if He is the Creator and gave laws, we need to follow those laws. The only way to be truly successful in life was to make Moses' laws of mount Sinai our life guides. Therefore, the 10 Commandments are our commandments from God. Their belief was that the history of the world was flowing through Jewish history. They also believed that God was in charge of a part of the Creator's plan (providence of God the Provider). That is why Ben Franklin said that God governed in the affairs of men.

Social Studies –

On the other hand, the 10 Commandments and Jewish History are simply events in time that unfolded. Possibly the amazing things in Egypt that happened to set the Jews free were natural occurrences that the Egyptians saw as God's hand, religious superstitions.

Therefore, we base our laws on the 10 Commandments but they are not divine. Our Founding Fathers believed them to be divine but we are smarter than that today. The Social Studies promoters do believe that the government of America, based on the Old Testament laws and God's Word, has been good for us, but they do not see them as divine guides. Yes, we based our laws on them and yes, they have served us well. But that doesn't mean we can't change them if we feel something else would serve man better.

3. Jesus

History—

History proclaims the person of Jesus Christ as the Creator's Son, sent to redeem man out of the fallen state left them by Adam and Eve's sin in the garden. They taught that the history of the world was all for the divine purpose of Jesus coming. Jesus was the reason we were here. Jesus' death and conquest over sin and death was the power that would change man's destiny. They taught that the person of Jesus was the great example we all should model. They believed that, if we were to get to Heaven, we must receive Him as our Savior. They believed that, if our children were to grow up to be productive, they must see Jesus as the divine example. They believed that, if government was to be run by people, the people in charge need to experience the person of Christ. Government, people and all our resources are to serve the purpose of this person, Jesus Christ.

Social Studies—

Social Studies, rather, sees Jesus Christ as simply another religious leader. He was a person that was killed by the Romans and it is *said* that He was raised from the dead.

Jesus' life has nothing to do with our lives today. He was a good man, a good teacher, and died for His cause, but has nothing to do with man's overall purpose. He was no different than other religious martyrs that gave their lives for their causes.

4. World Missions (Paul)

History—

The teachings of the past believed that the Apostle Paul of the Bible was the influence that brought about much of the world's expansion. The Great Commission given by Christ in Matthew 28:18-20 was the power that drove many to go into all the world. The Christian commitment to Missions motivated Columbus, the Pilgrims. Explorers, and others toward missions as a driving force.

Social Studies—

The teaching of today simply passes over the Commission given by Jesus Christ to Missions as simply another religious teaching that sometimes benefits peoples of the world. Some even go so far as to say, though, that missionaries do more harm than good, since they try to change cultures and end up doing a lot of damage. They say the missionaries should leave people to their beliefs, even when their average life expectancy is under 30 years of age, and filled with war, cannibalism, witchcraft and other detestable practices.

5. English Bible

History—

The teachings of the history teachers say that the translation of the English Bible was the factor that brought people together as well as drove people apart. The fight to translate the Bible into English was a driving force that influenced history in a tremendous way. Those men who were driven to translate the Word of God were hunted as criminals and killed if found by the Catholic Church. The Catholic Church did not want the common man to have the Bible in their own hands. This battle spanned over many continents. The English Bible coming to the common man drove people like the Pilgrims to sail for the New World to spread the Gospel to the Indians.

Social Studies—

Social Studies' teachings viewed the English Bible translation struggle as simply a struggle over religious power, and so they do not spend much time dealing with it. It simply happened.

6. Columbus

History—

History teachings of old saw Columbus as the hand of God. Columbus wrote in his person diary as he made the voyage to discover the New World that his men were afraid and wanted to turn back. He wrote that he was compelled by the Holy Spirit that kept him pushing forward. He wrote that he was on a mission to carry the Gospel of Christ to the unknowing world (The Great Commission).

Today, teachers inform their students that Columbus was searching for a new route to the Indies. He was financed by Ferdinand and Isabella for their purposes. Yes, to find the Indies route, but he also desired to carry the Catholic faith to new parts of the world. Columbus had a personal calling to carry Christ to the lost world, and his diary shows that. Out of 225 days, 72 entries in Columbus' log record a Christian reference. Of those 72 daily entries, there are over 100 different narratives. This works out to be one reference every third day!

Here's a systematic breakdown of entries which record Columbus' faith and the true purpose for his voyage:

23x – Acknowledges God's hand guiding events
19x – Gives praise and or thanks to God

13x – Seeks and pleads for conversion of natives
11x – Describes his men and homeland as Christian
8x – Seeks strength from God to carry on
7x – Maintains Holy Days and prayers
5x – Gives Christian names to geographic features
5x – Commits himself and enterprise to God
3x – Desires profiles to be used for Christ
1x – Recognizes Satan's attempt to stop voyage

Social Studies—

Social Studies teachings of today teach that Columbus was on a mission to find gold and a new route to the Indies. They treat Columbus as a pirate-type that simply was out to serve himself. Most of us who were educated in this Social Studies way never even *heard* of the Columbus diary nor his words.

7. Pilgrims

History—

History examined the Pilgrims from a Great Commission perspective. The Pilgrims were driven by the Great Commission of Christ and a desire to get their children away from the worldly influence of the English and Catholics. Their belief in God and the Great Commission was very evident in the Mayflower Compact.

The History teachers of the past explained the storm that the Mayflower experienced that changed their course from Jamestown to the area north that became Massachusetts Bay, as the hand of God giving them a fresh start since the Jamestown Colony was not motivated as much by Christian principles.

Social Studies—

Social Studies teaching of today teaches that the Pilgrims were looking for religious freedom from English Catholics or Church of England oppressors. This is not true. The Pilgrims went to Holland first and had religious freedom there. But they were compelled to come to the New World because of the Great Commission.

They teach that, when they were flown off course, this was simply a weather happening. They even teach that at Thanksgiving the Pilgrims were thanking the Indians for all their help, when in truth they were very specifically thinking God, who was the great provider.

You see the difference? To thank the Indians was to thank man and ignore the hand of God. But to thank God for His provision was to say that God takes part in our lives (providence). Can you see how important the view we take of history is? There is a dramatic difference made in our children's presuppositions about life as they learn that God is the Provider.

8. Patriots

History—

History teaches that the patriots were driven by faith and a belief that God was their protector and provider. They taught that the patriots were Christian gentlemen with a commission and a mission. They were guided by the hand of God. The history teachers spent a lot of time teaching the students that God was involved in the founding and the forming of America. They spent a lot of time researching the amazing miracles of the Revolutionary War and how God used clouds, rain, fog, etc. They also taught the great stories of George Washington and how God just powerfully protected him. They explained how God was in this country's beginning and how we as Americans are part of God's plan. That is why we hear the words in the seldom-sung verse of our National Anthem:

> *Blest with vict'ry and peace, may the heav'n rescued land praise the Pow'r that hath made and preserved us a nation!*
> *Then conquer we must, when our cause it is just; and this be our motto: "In God we trust!"*

I wonder what kind of song would be written today if the National Anthem was to be written by the Social Studies crowd.

Social Studies teachings on the other hand tell our children that these great leaders were men of lust, pride and problems. They teach that these men did some wonderful things, but in no way were they men to be honored as the past historians believed them to be. They tell our students that George Washington was a man of many lusts when, in truth, Mr. Washington, though not a perfect man, was a man of prayer, honor and godly character.

The difference in the two approaches to what kind of men the patriots were, and what they did for our nation is extreme. The truth is, the Social Studies teachers cannot teach the truth of history because the truth about the patriots was full of prayer, Bible promotion, exalting God, etc. If the truth is told, God is exalted. Therefore, if God cannot be promoted in government schools, the truth cannot be told in government schools, because the truth of the patriots is filled with their belief in the providence of God. They believed God was the Creator of America. They believed America to be the new chosen people. It's hard for a Social Studies teacher to teach history because of the "no God' dilemma.

Therefore, the new generations have lost their respect for the Founding Fathers and their patriotism as well. They simply see America as another country founded and fought for by men who were selfishly motivated.

9. Pioneers

History—

The pioneer era was an era filled with excitement for the history reader. The pioneer era covered times of westward expansion, laying of the railroad tracks, development of industries and of the great plantations of the South, fighting in the Civil Way, and much more.

History will tell the story with a belief that God was walking with man to help him, to guide him. History will point out the Great Awakening Two and how a time of preaching and a revival time affected the expansion westward.

History will tell the story of Abraham Lincoln with respect and admiration. He believed strongly, along with the other founders of our great nation, in true civic education (not the propaganda that so often comprises the Social Studies' view of civic education). Children learning to live within the constraints of, and a respect for, laws. Learning a love for their country and the truth about those who gave so much to establish it. These things being just as important as simply learning the ABC's. Here is a quote by Abraham Lincoln on the importance of civic education in a speech given to the Young Men's Lyceum of Springfield, IL, on January 27, 1837:

> *Let reverence for the laws be*
> *breathed by every American mother to*
> *the lisping babe that prattles on her*

lap. Let it be taught in schools, in seminaries, and in colleges. Let it be written in primers, spelling books, and in almanacs. Let it be preached from the pulpit, proclaimed in legislative halls, and enforced in the courts of justice. And, in short, let it become the political religion of the nation.[xxxv]

Social Studies—

Social Studies will tell the story of expansion in a way that only emphasizes the hunger for gold, land and adventure. It is true that gold, land and adventure were a part of the pioneer era, but not the only part.

Social Studies only emphasizes the greed of man and his drive to be selfish. History is able to tell of greed and his selfishness, but history can continue and tell of men who were, in turn, rocks of that time; men who were tremendous men of character, because of their Christian values and biblical beliefs.

Social Studies sometimes is very hard on great men of character, such as Abraham Lincoln, who was without a doubt a tremendous Christian man, with a great prayer life, and a leader in Christian virtue. But Social Studies cannot tell of that part of Lincoln.

Social Studies can only *say* a man has good character. History can *explain why* a man has character. Example: Social Studies tells the stories of great Americans and events in facts, figures, and dates along. But History tells of character and heart and rich personalities. It tells of sinners and why they were so, and godly men and why they were so. In truth, Social Studies of our day is simply only *half* the story. The writers have been forbidden to tell the rest of the story because of its religious teaching. In truth we cannot study American History in its entirety without getting a good Bible lesson, and a lesson in Christian character.

Christian character, respect for authority and our laws, and an appreciation for our rich Christian history are very important elements needed among youth, but how will they possess these treasures unless they are taught? They cannot learn in a government school class room, unless they can have it and not mention the Bible or Jesus Christ, and that of course is impossible. The way the story of the past is told in the 1990s is only *part* of the truth. Such a tragedy.

10. Present Time

History—

History from 1900-2021 is told with excitement and tragedy. Our youth will be challenged to look into the stories of the wars, the industrial revolution and successes and failures in man's war over conscious with the view from God's seat. History will challenge our students to look at facts and learn from our past to affect our future. Present-time history of the 20th century is filled with great discoveries. If the story of the

20th century were being taught by the tutors of our Founding Fathers, they would see the hand of God in the unfolding of the great discoveries of the 20th century. They would challenge the student to look at what has happened and see how God can allow them to fit into this great time and be used to promote good and godliness. Simply, the challenge is to the student to be an instrument of God for the good of man and the promotion of the work of God.

Social Studies—

Social Studies, on the other hand, simply approaches the discoveries, successes and failures as chance unfolding and happenings that were motivated by man's greed and ambition. They simply do not discuss what caused that man or woman to have the greed or ambition. Social Studies' only challenge to the student is to go forth and make a name for yourself, to get your piece of the pie. But the motivation is totally wrong. They are challenged to do so with only self in mind. Make a name for yourself, get your piece of the pie. Self, self, self. You, you, you. Yours, yours, yours.

Some who read this would say this is exaggerated. I say compare the two books and then look at society and tell me that I am exaggerating. I say to the person who would say that this is an exaggeration, you just simply do not want to face the truth. This is truth, simply cause and effect.

Let me illustrate my point: Regarding Thanksgiving, the old history books told us of the Pilgrims' gratitude to God for His giving them a good harvest. "Our first Thanksgiving was, of course, held by the Pilgrims in the fall of 1621. Washington's Thanksgiving Proclamation (on October 3, 1789) was our first national Thanksgiving. Abraham Lincoln in 1863 made it an annual national holiday to be celebrated on the last Thursday in November. Originally it was a day of thanks and prayer and supplication and request for divine blessing."[xxxvi]

The Social Studies books teach simply that the Pilgrims were thankful to the Indians for all their help. How far we have come that our Thanksgiving celebrations of the present are often reduced to indulgence in turkey, parades, and shopping.

I hope you can see the difference and the effect of the difference. This is only one story, but the whole of history has been altered to leave out any references or gratitude to a Holy God for His help. This is a comparison of the approach to our history the way our Founding Fathers approached it as opposed to the way our children approach it. As we understand this difference, I hope you can see the reason the people of today respond so differently to life.

I hope you can see why our Founding Fathers had character and wisdom, and why our leaders of today seem to be lacking in many needed qualities for great leadership.

IV. THE FRUITS OF TWO TEACHING MODELS

In this section I hope to be able to help you with a few valuable qualities, attitudes or character traits being lost or gained, depending on how history is taught. I believe the facts and figures approach to our past is causing our future generations to lose important personality traits that once brought us a great nation.

To receive or to lose valuable quality traits, that is the question.

Let's take just a few character qualities and examine the gain and loss in Wave Two.

1. *Man's Self Value/Self Esteem*

Man is important – Man is not just a life in time that happened and it's gone. Man was created by God for a purpose. Man is important to God. God cares for man; therefore, man is important. Man is God's personal creation, made in the image of God.

This quality is important because we are a part of an eternal, holy, powerful Creator, God. We are a part of His holy work and will. God, in His providence, is involved in the lives of men. God cares for you, created you, and was willing to die for you.

This is the approach of history, Providence that once was a part of the school materials presented in Science and History class. It is no wonder we developed such leaders as Noah Webster, John Adams, George Washington, etc.

But, if this approach is changed to a strictly factional Social Studies approach, no God is involved, and man is an elevated animal. It is no wonder we continue to need to offer self-esteem classes to help students with their opinion of themselves.

Help! Man's value is missing!

2. Eternal Existence

Man is eternal—Man is a part of God; therefore, we live forever. The quality of life is extremely affected by an eternal appointment, if man knows that he has an eternal appointment with his Creator. This appointment will be a time after death when he will give an account for the way he has lived his life; therefore, he looks at life much differently. He develops an extreme drive to live a life that will be something to look forward to accounting for. The Founding Fathers' view of God was such that they knew they couldn't measure up to God, but at least they knew the day of accounting was coming.

Help! Eternity has been stolen!

Without this appointment in the student's heart, the accountability factor is gone. Therefore, eat, drink and be merry, for tomorrow we cease to exist.

3. Positive Role Models

A study of biblical heroes gives character, purpose, and supplies role models that will teach a student how to be blessed and how to fail without failing.

The story of Noah is a story of God calling a man to dedicate his life to serve all of creation, a man willing to go forth and do, in the voices of laughter, God's will.

Moses was a called leader to deliver his people from bondage; a man called by God for a specific time and appointment.

David teaches us how to be a king and serve others as well as God. David teaches us the great side of success and the hard side of failures.

Daniel was a man in a strange land with convictions, courage and a calling to stand, even in the face of lions, for what he believed. Daniel did so as a godly Christian gentleman. Even his opposing king came to love him.

Jesus is the ultimate loving man's man, the ultimate leader, the ultimate God-man, the ultimate person.

Heroes are a very important part of life. Everyone has heroes. All of our children need good, godly heroes. The people our students hold up as heroes are whom they try to model. Think of the heroes of our children today and you will see why we are in such a shape.

We need to return to heroes with godly character.

Help! Our heroes are missing character!

4. Inward Emotions of Good

Love—Love is described by the Bible with differing words, but every word for love denotes giving, caring and sacrifice. Whether or not we experience God's love through Jesus Christ affects whether or not we can love with a pure heart.

The love I am talking about is pure love.

If we have no Jesus in our lives, we have no love in our lives. I am sure some might say, "I know people who are not Christians but do love." This may be true, but they are running on the influence taught them by the society Jesus built. The farther we get away from Jesus, the farther away you get from love. He is the source of love. No Jesus, no love! Any place love is not is a type of Hell.

Help! Pure love is rapidly disappearing!

5. Outward Expressions of Love

Sacrifice—Sacrifice is giving of self or giving self for another. Jesus sacrificed Himself for the sins of the world. An animal is sacrificed daily in order that we can eat him and live. This happens daily at meal time. This was introduced that we would understand the picture of sacrifice. Therefore, when Jesus was willing to give himself we could understand the truth of sacrifice and what it meant. In truth meat eaters are reminded of the sacrifice of Jesus daily when at the dinner table. Vegetarians are reminded of the resurrection daily as they enjoy a meal. It's simply amazing that God hinged our total existence on a continual reminder of the sacrifice of Jesus and the resurrection when we sit down at the dinner table. Plant a seed in the ground and it comes up to bear new life.

Sacrificing for others is a big part of our lives—if we truly love.

Years ago our grandparents were willing to sacrifice their comfort for future generations. We must search hard and long to find that type of sacrificing spirit in the world today. But if, when you find love and sacrifice, you will find God, and the person of Jesus. When we lost Jesus, the ultimate Teacher of sacrifice, we lost the special quality of sacrifice.

Help! Sacrificial people are disappearing fast!

6. Natural Qualities of Good

Character—Defined: A mark by cutting or engraving, to cut or engrave, a lasting mark. This is one use and the base use. Character is peculiar qualities, impressed by nature or habits of a person that distinguishes him from others.

Thus, we say a character is not formed when the person has not acquired stable and distinctive qualities. In fact, unless he has stable, engrafted, good qualities, he has no character.

Character is a great quality that is rapidly disappearing.

Remember the story of George Washington and the cherry tree? Our children today scarcely ever hear this story. But it once was told of Washington because he had character. He was honest. He had a conscience, etc.

Character—how can we live at peace and in prosperity without it? We will only bring back character when our students choose and model heroes with character.

Help! Character is disappearing fast!

7. Concrete Convictions

Absolute Truth—Truth that is absolute; truth that is beyond question. Absolute truth always comes up missing when the Bible becomes a book in question.

The Bible is the truth, the ultimate, unmovable truth, the only truth that is not up for debate. This is the way our Founding Fathers viewed the Bible. Therefore, they were confident in what was right or wrong. The question was not, "What does the majority think?" The question was, "What does the Bible say?"

First, evolution had undermined the creation story, and then other areas of the Bible began to be in question.

If the Bible is not true, there are no absolute truths. History is told through the eyes of the teller without the foundation of the Bible. Science is taught through the eyes of an evolutionist science teacher and is continually changing with new discoveries. Other subjects are the same, depending on who's telling the story.

But the Bible has been and still is absolute truth. With absolute truth comes absolute confidence, absolute right and wrong, absolute values and absolute morals, etc.

Without biblical truth, absolute truth is gone; therefore, absolute authority is gone as well.

With the lack of authority and absolute confidence comes and absolutely insecure people, a people blown around with every wind that blows. Truth continues to change with whoever is talking. Therefore, big trouble.

Help! Absolute truth is missing!

8. Right and Wrong

Morals—Defined: Morals are from manners. Relating to the practice, manners or conduct of men as social beings in relation to each other. The word "moral" is applicable to actions that are good or evil, or virtuous, and has reference to the law of God as the standard by which their character is to be determined.

Morality is a quality that is only present where the Bible is absolute truth. Today, people continue to change with time and influence. Therefore, absolute morals are absent where the Bible is questions.

Without morals sin abounds, and where sin abounds so do diseases, pain, problems, sorrows and even death. It's simply cause and effect.

Help! Morals are missing!

9. More than Knowledge

Wisdom—Wisdom is a word that is not talked about much these days. Wisdom is seeing the root of the problem rather than just the symptoms of the problem. Wisdom is the ability to look beyond that is seen from the surface. Therefore, more than knowledge, wisdom is God-given.

A man cannot truly have wisdom without seeing the problem through the eyes of God the

Creator. Since God created us and is ultimate knowledge, He knows all there is to know about everything. The only way to have wisdom is to have wisdom come to you by developing divine eyes. This, of course, comes only by the divine Word of God and a divine Helper, God.

Wisdom is almost gone today. Therefore, our political leaders and authorities make decisions that ultimately cause so much damage. You truly cannot see cause and effect well without God-given wisdom.

When our Founding Fathers put together our government, it is evident divine wisdom was present. But when divine wisdom is gone, bad decisions are inevitable.

Wisdom has been stolen! The thief is the humanistic approach to education.

Help! Wisdom has been stolen!

10. Respect of Others

Reverence—Reverence and respect go hand in hand. Reverence is truly rendering respect to an authority or person.

Reverence or respect is a fruit of admiring a person or holding someone in highest esteem. If our students view their fellow man as elevated animals, they view their teachers as people who cannot agree, if truths are changing weekly, if leaders are challengeable, if God is none existent, then there really is no reason to respect because you cannot respect what you do not admire.

Help!   Reverence and respect are disappearing rapidly! Stolen!

11. Reason to Live

Purpose—Purpose is simply a person's reason for existing.

Your purpose can only be as good as the way you view your importance to society and to God's ultimate plan for the ages. Your importance is only as big as your view of God and His providence.

No God, no future. No future, no purpose.

History (His Story) involves man with eternal God and eternal purposes and destination, the heavenly city. If the destination of the heavenly city is gone, the eternal purpose is gone. If there is no God, if the Bible is not true, then we are on our own. Man is only as big as his Creator. If his Creator is man, he is man-sized. If man is God's creation, he has God-sized potential.

If God doesn't exist, man has only the things of the world to live for. After he sees that this world's goods do not satisfy, he has nowhere else to go. Therefore, he has no purpose.

But when God, Heaven and heavenly crowns are waiting, the throne of God is the limit. Therefore, dream big!

Our Founding Fathers had a heavenly vision; therefore, this life was step one on the way to step two, Heaven.

Help! Purpose is missing!

12. Driven to Attain

Ambition—Defined: A person's drive to seek or go forth and make life interesting. Ambition is an inward drive to success or to be successful in life.

Ambition is a result of purpose. If purpose is missing, ambition is missing. You cannot have high ambition without high purpose. Your ambition is limited to your view of your purpose.

Simply, you can only reach as far as your eyes can focus.

Help! Ambition is missing!

13. Voice of Conviction

Conscience—Defined: Self or inner knowledge, self-judgment of right or wrong. Power within to decide lawful or lawless actions, the inner voice of morality.

The conscience is a voice inside that shouts stop and go when decisions are being made. However, without absolute truth the conscience is confused and without fuel. Without the Bible there are no absolute truth. Therefore, no Bible, no science. We are missing biblical truth and biblical truth is the source of man's conscience. The conscience is what gives man the ability to govern himself without outside governing powers. People with a biblical, healthy conscience don't need policemen to guard them to keep them from doing wrong.

A nation that loses its conscience spends a lot of money on policemen and jails. I rest my case.

Help! Conscience is missing!

These are only a few of the qualities we are missing as a result of the new view of God and His Word. I know you can think of many more missing valuables. The need is there and growing.

Let's move on. I would like to show you what I believe to be a conspiracy to erase God from society totally, and ultimately destroy our great country. Please read on and see if I am not right.

14. Committed to God's America—We call this Patriotism

Patriotism Defined: A person who loves or is in zealous support and defense of his own country or country's interest.

Benjamin Rush (1745-1813), was a physician, a signer of the Declaration of Independence, the "father of public schools" and a principal promoter of the American Sunday School Union. In 1798, after the adoption of the Constitution, He declared that the only foundation for a republic is laid in religion. Without this there can be no virtue, and without virtue there can be no liberty, and liberty is the object and life of all republican governments. He shares here some of his thoughts on what patriotism means— how it incorporates both a moral and religious duty. To his fellow countrymen:

> *Patriotism is as much a virtue as justice, and is as necessary for the support of societies as natural affection is for the support of families. The Amor Patriae is both a moral and a religious duty. It comprehends not only the love of our neighbors but of millions of our fellow creatures, not only of the present but of future generations. This virtue we find constitutes a part of the first characters in history. The holy men of old, in proportion as they possessed a religious were endowed with public spirit. What did not Moses forsake and suffer for his countrymen! What shining examples of Patriotism do we behold in Joshua,*

Samuel, Maccabeus, and all the illustrious princes, captains, and prophets amongst the Jews! St. Paul almost wishes himself accursed for his countrymen and kinsmen after the flesh. Even our Saviour himself gives a sanction to this virtue. He confined his miracles and gospel at first to his own country.[xxxvii]

When patriotism is high, so is a willingness to sacrifice for country. Great examples of this are evident in many of the instances surrounding the Revolutionary War. One instance is Patrick Henry's speech at St. John's Church, March 23, 1775.

This is one of the most famous speeches of the revolutionary era and helped infuse the citizens of Virginia with a sense of national spirit. With the growing presence of British forces in the colonies, Patrick Henry introduced a set of resolutions for organizing and arming a state militia and putting the colony of Virginia on defensive footing. The church in which Henry gave the speech was packed, and the windows were thrown open to allow more people to hear. When Henry finished, his fellow delegates, who included Jefferson and Washington, sat in awed silence.

We have petitioned—we have remonstrated—we have supplicated—we have prostrated ourselves before the throne, and have implored its interposition to arrest the tyrannical hands of the ministry and parliament. Our petitions have been slighted; our remonstrances have produced additional violence and insult; our supplications have been disregarded; and we have been spurned, with contempt, from the foot of the throne. In vain, after these things, may we indulge the fond hope of peace and reconciliation. There is no longer any room for hope. If we wish to be free—if we mean to preserve inviolate those inestimable privileges for which we have been so long contending—if we mean not basely to abandon the noble struggle in which we have been so long engaged, and which we have pledged ourselves never to abandon, until the glorious object of our contest shall be obtained—we must fight!—I repeat it, sire, we must fight!! An appeal to arms and to the God of hosts, is all that is left us!

"They tell us, sir," continued Mr. Henry, "that we are weak—unable to cope with so formidable an adversary. But when shall we be stronger? Will it be the next week or the next year? Will it be when we are totally disarmed, and when a British guard shall be stationed in every house? Shall we gather strength by irresolution and inaction? Shall we acquire the means of effectual

resistance by living supinely on our backs, and hugging the delusive phantom of hope, until our enemies shall have bound us hand and foot? Sir, we are not weak, if we make a proper use of those means which the God of nature hath placed in our power. Three millions of people armed in the holy cause of liberty, and in such a country as that which we possess, are invincible by any force which our enemy can send against us. Besides, sir, we shall not fight our battles alone. There is a just God who presides over the destines of nations, and who will raise up friends to fight our battles for us. The battle, sir, is not to the strong alone; it is to the vigilant, the active, the brave. Besides, sir, we have no election. If we were base enough to desire it, it is now too late to retire from the contest. There is no retreat but in submission and slavery! Our chains are forged. Their clanking may be heard on the plains of Boston! The war is inevitable—and let it some!! I repeat it, sir, let it come!!!

"It is vain, sir, to extenuate the matter. Gentlemen may cry, peace, peace—but there is not peace. The war is actually begun! The next gale that sweeps from the north will bring to our ears the clash of resounding *arms! Our brethren are already in the field! Why stand we here idle! What is it that gentlemen wish? What would they have? Is life so dear, or peace so sweet, as to be purchased at the price of chains and slavery? Forbid it, Almighty!—I know not what course others may take; but as for me," cried he, with both arms extended aloft, his brows knit, every feature marked with the resolute purpose of his soul, and his voice swelled to its boldest note of exclamation—"give me liberty, or give me death!"* xxxviii

We are suffering from the lack of such patriotism because we are suffering from a lack of faith—faith in God, faith in God's providence, etc.

Patriotism is fast disappearing, because providence is disappearing. Patriotism runs from fuels called faith, providence and a willingness to sacrifice. We simply cannot expect our people to be willing to sacrifice even until death without God as our Provider, Protector, etc. We cannot expect a people that live for self to be committed to sacrifice for others! These patriots were a people who believed that we were created in the image of God, created with a purpose and a cause, created and called into a great commission. Therefore, they believed in their country; they were true Patriots. How can we get true patriots from the foundations our country is now built upon? Our children grow up being told they are a product of chance and without a future.

Therefore, they should live every day for pleasure and self-gratification. There is no God. There is no afterlife. There is no Creator. There is no Great Commission. There is no providence.

Therefore, we lose when God is taken from our future generations of leaders. It's simple cause and effect!

Let's go forward and examine just a few of the subtle and mandated disappearances. There are many, but this is a summary, and I hope you will examine others on your own.

V. PRESENT DAY PROBLEMS FROM "FORGETTING" GOD

The disappearance problem comes really in two forms.

1. *Cause and Effect*

If man rejects God, we will be affected. The humanist (man worshipper) is conspiring to remove any reference to God from American society. This is and will result in a new generation forgetting where they came from, who made them, and who and what they are. Simple cause and effect. Erase the biblical foundations and the structure will fall. It's hard to imagine people with any intelligence at all not being able to see the effect this vacancy will cause on America, but a desire to sin seems to cause blindness.

2. *God's Hedge will disappear*

The God of America has placed a hedge of protection around our nation. We have never experienced the major catastrophes that many other nations have. Our government, which is a Constitutional Republic, is a longstanding declaration of God's favor toward us. The worst things that have happened to America have been the Civil War, a few Stock Market crashes, and the attacks on our Twin Towers and Pentagon on September 11, 2001. That could change any day.

We were a nation built on righteousness. But when America erases God from their society, the Bible from their ultimate truth, and the person of Jesus as their companion, then replace all these with the humanist's worship of man, then we see 35 million abortions, pornography, homosexuality, etc. We see our people living for lust and reaping the consequences of such a life without God.

We fear now that God will allow us to be cursed because of our sin. God will be compelled to judge us for our unrighteous living publicly paraded daily. Terrorism, germs, diseases, etc., are very possible and almost inevitably in our future if God has removed His hedge of protection. The tragedies are coming if we choose to be a nation that doesn't need God.

Natural disasters, weather disasters, financial disaster, etc., the possibilities are endless, without God's protection and blessings.

We have erased our allegiance to the Creator. What can we expect? The conspiracy is in place; the results are starting to surface.

Let me discuss just a few examples of the conspiracy to erase God from American society. Some forms are subtle, some are ordered by the court systems.

o *Our Creator has disappeared, therefore the virtues, values, character, honesty, conscience, etc., is missing and more godly qualities are vanishing daily.*

o *Providence (God involved in providing for us and guiding us with His hand)—The providence of God is valuable and, without it, we are just another people without a purpose.*

o *Public references to God and His involvement are missing. Let's examine a few specific cases.*

The Liberty Bell—A Subtle Change

Fifty years of God's peace and prosperity elapsed over Pennsylvania after William Penn's 1701 Charter of Privilege to his colonists. In 1751, the year of Jubilee, the Pennsylvania Assembly ordered a commemorative bell to be cast in England, for the anniversary of Penn's Charter. That is the bell now known as the famed Liberty Bell. Speaker of the Assembly, Isaac Norris, himself a Quaker, chose a portion of Leviticus 25:10 for the inscription of the bell: "...proclaim liberty throughout the land unto all the inhabitants thereof."

It was in the steeple tower of Independence Hall that the famed old bell was rung to proclaim American Independence. This symbol of American freedom and democracy rang for all the major landmarks of our nation's history, until in 1835, while tolling the requiem for Chief Justice Marshall, it cracked. In 1835, the bell was lowered to a spot directly below the tower. The full verse from Leviticus 25:10 was then inscribed upon its base: "And ye shall hallow the fiftieth year, and proclaim liberty throughout all the land unto all the inhabitants thereof."

For years, the Liberty Bell was housed in Independence Hall where it had originally hung, but at midnight, on the first of January, 1976, despite great protest by patriotic and tradition-loving Philadelphia, the famed old bell was moved from Independence Hall to an ultra-modern structure across the street. It is unfortunate that the historic base of the Liberty Bell, which included the full verse from Leviticus 25:10 is no longer on display. This foremost symbol of American Independence is now interpreted in the Independence National Historic Park overseers as "a symbol of world freedom," rather than what its *true* Christian history indisputably proclaims: "And ye shall hallow the fiftieth year, and proclaim liberty throughout all the land unto all the inhabitants thereof."[xxxix]

Now tell me how anyone with truly a love for history could just remove such a foundation from such a historical bell and simply disregard it. It is beyond me to understand if I simply look at this fact through eyes of logic. If the humanistic, no God people have their way, all these reminders will disappear. It makes sense if I know of their goal is to remove God.

The Conversion of Pocahontas—A Subtle Removal

Immortalized in Jamestown, Virginia history is the life and conversion of Pocahontas, the "Christian Indian Princess." She was the favorite daughter of Powhatan, who ruled the Powhatan Confederacy. She was born about 1595, probably at Woronocomoco, 16 miles from Jamestown. She had saved Captain John Smith's life twice during the colony's first years. In 1608-1609 she was a frequent and welcome visitor to Jamestown. After accepting Jesus Christ as Savior, Pocahontas was baptized into the Christian faith in the original church at Jamestown in 1613. A beautiful oil painting capturing this event hangs within the U.S. Capitol Rotunda. She subsequently married John Rolfe, Council Member of the Jamestown Colony.

A replica of the only known original extant portrait of Pocahontas hangs on a wall adjacent to the gift shop at the Visitors' Center in Jamestown, which is run by the National Park Service, Department of the Interior. It depicts this Indian princess as she appeared when presented to the Queen, in royal English attire. Painted by the artist Brooke, it immortalizes her for Indian heritage and her conversion to Christianity.

The inscription under the painting reads "Motoaksa als Rebecca, daughter of the mighty Prince Powhatan Emperor of Attanoughknowmouck at Virginia converted and baptized into the Christian faith, and wife to John Rolfe."

It's interesting that a duplicate version of this portrait is available for purchase in the National Park service Visitor's Center gift shop. However, significantly, the inscription under the image has been rewritten. Lacking, of course, is her conversion to Christianity.[xl]

George Washington—A Subtle Disappearance

George Washington was once pictured as a man of Christian faith and a man of prayer. But recently his pictures, prayers and references to God have been conveniently left out.

Deuteronomy 28—A Subtle Disappearance

The Bible was opened to this chapter and the President's hand placed upon it when he took his oath of office. The Bible would be opened to this chapter where blessings were promised to a nation who honored God and cursing was promised to a nation that didn't honor Him. The Bible is rapidly disappearing from these very important events. This seems to be a small thing, but what does this say to God? What does it say about those running our country? Subtle changes always seem to say to God that His promises are not important to America any longer.

The Bible and the Court Room—A Subtle Disappearance

Once we placed our hand on a Bible in the court room as we took the witness stand. Once we said, "I will tell the truth, so help me, God." All these subtle changes. The Bible is not there, and the oath doesn't mention God in most court rooms. Prayers and Bible reading were removed from schools in 1963, by a court room mandate. The Ten Commandments were removed from school in the 1980s by a court room mandate.

Many other battles are being fought daily. I think you can see the continual pattern. Some are subtle and some are mandated by the courts of our land. One might say, "Who are these people who are continually fussing and fighting to get God's name, His picture, and His Word or influence out of our sight? And why are they doing this?"

I have simply inserted a few of the very plentiful illustrations of the subtle removals as well as the court room mandated removals of Christian heritage and the rewriting of our history. Some might say, "Why would this be happening?" or, "You must be exaggerating." Those who would have a hard time believing that there is a conspiracy to erase God from America are those who do not know the agenda of the humanists and their enforces, the ACLU. Let me just tell you what the ACLU's agenda is.

The hidden agenda of the "American Civil Liberties Union" (a.k.a. the ACLU) from which the following is quoted:

- *Policy No. 81 calls for a permanent ban on displays of the nativity scene and the memorial on public property.*
- *Policy No. 84 calls for the removal of "under God" from the Pledge of Allegiance to the flag and the Republic for which it stands.*
- *Policy No. 92 calls for an end to tax exemption for all churches and synagogues.*
- *Policy No. 210 calls for the legalization of all narcotics, including crack and angel dust, contending "the introduction of substances into one's own body" is a civil liberty.*

With a secret membership of 250,000, the ACLU is a vastly-changed organization from the one Roger Baldwin presided over in the 1950s. Today, its ideology patterns the ACLU's ideology of the 1930s from which John Dewey resigned because of Marxist domination.

The monuments to the ACLU are now all around us, superseding and removing the monuments and memorials to America's greatness—her true history, representing the One Nation under God. The public school system is a classic example of this phenomenon: The Lord's Prayer (Matthew 6); the Ten Commandments (Exodus 20); and the scene of the birth of our Lord and Savior Jesus Christ (Luke 2) are prohibited in those schools, courtesy of the ACLU.[xli]

When a flood covers an area like a blanket, the effects are always evident. When a mighty wave unfolds on the coastal beach, the ruins are left. Cause and effect are like the rains, floods or waves. There is always an effect to a cause.

What we are trying to get people to understand is a simple fact that is very evident in every area of life, cause and effect. If you plant a crop, you get the harvest of seeds that you planted. Whatsoever a man sows that shall he also reap, cause and effect.

Those who continually try to change society to be absent from God's influence try to deny this very evident truth. They try to say it will not affect society in the negative. But just a little altering of words affects us greatly, and the secular humanists know it. They just do not want to admit it in Christian words. Let me illustrate— Drug Free School Zones! This is a statement that they hope will discourage drug dealers and students from any drug use on school property— Don't Drink and Drive! They are hoping that these words spoken enough will deter drinking and driving—Get Met; It Pays! This is a commercial statement made with great expense to the insurance company to try to get you and me to use their insurance.

It's very clear that the secular world believes in cause and effect. Just look at the commercial industry and the millions of dollars spent on cause-and-effect words and picture commercials. They do believe in it. But when it comes to the effects of the Bible, Jesus, godly patriots, godly heroes influencing our children, when it comes to admitting the effects of no God school zones, they just turn their heads. It is like the smoker who knows the truth about smoking, but closes his mind to the truth, because he is so hooked on the flavor of a smoke, he can't admit the truth. But the effects don't stop because he ignores the truth. Smoking, drinking, drugs, etc., they all have a cause and effect. The effect is always death and destruction. If that is true, why doesn't the hooked person quit or, better yet, not start? The fact is, sin is fun for a season—that's the draw, but it also carries with it a large consequence—that's the danger. The only question is, are we willing to pay the price for having no Bible, no Creator, no Christian history, and no biblical stability? The disappearances of these are affecting us greatly!

The disappearance problem will affect us in two ways. 1. Cause and effect—If we take God out of society, we will suffer the effects of that mistake. But the second effect of a no-God society is even more troubling than the first. 2. The loss of God's promised blessings. Our blessings of the past have been a result of our claiming Deuteronomy 28, God's promised blessings and God-warned curses. Our blessings have come from God. God has, in the past, built a hedge of protection around America. All we have done He seems to have smiled upon. Therefore, God has "shed His grace on thee," from whence comes the line from *America the Beautiful*. Our blessings come from God's hedge about us and His smiling on us. Our successes are a result of obeying God's words of instruction. But the last half of Deuteronomy 28 is a warning to the nation of His that turns from Him. Therefore, a curse comes to those who reject Him.

Summary

Cause and Effect—simple and true, but simply ignored for the sake of sinners. In truth, the desire to get away from God and His teachings has sacrificed the truths of cause and effect. They totally ignore the impact that will be made on a people that choose to live without God and the Bible. A people separated from God and the Bible have no conscience, no love, no future, and no godly qualities or character. Closing our eyes to the effects does not erase the effects. Therefore, we are in the shape we are in when it comes to character, etc.

The simple fact is, removing the wonder of the Creator and replacing Him with a mud pit affects us in devastating fashion.

Removing reference to God from our founding removes our importance, our purpose, etc. We simply become a ship floating without any reason. It simply puts us in just a place in time without real importance. Eat, drink and merry, for tomorrow we die. Therefore, the only reason to live becomes today and self-enjoyment. No eternal purpose. So sad.

Truth, character, virtue, morals, ethics, conscience—all these are without fuel apart from the Bible. If you try to say a nation should have these qualities without the Bible it's like saying a combustion engine should run without gas. The fuel is simply not present to motivate it to run. It's simply a case of cause and effect.

That is why John Adams said, "Our Constitution was made for a moral and religious people. It is wholly inadequate to the government of any other." He said this in an address to the military, on October 11, 1798.

Our government was created with the expectations that the Bible would be taught to our people and people could be trusted to govern themselves. They believed the Bible would give our people a conscience. But when the conscience goes, more and more laws need to be passed and freedoms are lost.

The sin nature is already present in every man. The sin nature brings destructive attitudes of selfishness and greed. Sacrifice, love, and giving spirit are taught and developed with the help of God. Just watch a child. Even an infant has the selfish tendencies, me, me, me, mine, mine, mine. This only is changed by teaching and a working of God in their lives.

We need God's help, because morals, virtue, honesty, conscience, etc., are sadly missing! The thief is a humanistic, no-God education and society.

What can we do? We know what is missing. We know what causes it to be missing. We must replace the missing pieces of God's Word, God and Christ in order to give back the fuel for morality and good. Will we or will we not do so? That is the question!

This is the *second* wave!

Let's move on to wave three.

_____
_____
_____

CHAPTER THREE

THE THIRD WAVE
WATERING DOWN THE WORD

If the foundations be destroyed,
what can the righteous do?
-- PSALM 11:3

I.   THE TIDAL WAVE TO COME!

The winter of 1997-98 brought much rain to the west coast of the United States. Houses had the foundations washed out from under them. The news pictures daily showed what happens when the foundation is taken from under any structures, total self-destruction. The greatest architects in the world cannot save a structure that has lost its foundation. Millions of dollars were spent in California trying to keep the rain from taking the rest of the foundations. All the architects with all their knowledge could do nothing but sit and watch once the foundation was gone. They sat watching as very expensive homes simply fell apart and into valleys and into the ocean. This is a picture of what happens when the foundations are removed. This is a great example of our theme passage for this study, Psalm 11:3, "If the foundation be destroyed, what can the righteous do?"

This is also a great testimony to the words of Jesus when He said in Matthew 7:24-27:

Therefore, whosoever heareth these sayings of mine, and doeth them, I will liken him unto a wise man, which built his house upon a rock: And the rain descended, and the floods came, and the winds blew, and beat upon that house; and it fell not: for it was founded upon a rock. And every one that heareth these sayings of mine, and doeth them not, shall be likened unto a foolish man, which built his house upon the sand: And the rain descended, and the floods came, and the winds blew, and beat upon that house; and it fell: and great was the fall of it.

The first two waves of foundation erasing have been hard on America. These two erasings have left us staggering with much devastation as a result. The first two needed to be in place as a prerequisite to the third. The third wave will be the most devastating of all. The Word of God is the foundation of all truth. Therefore, America is the house about to fall into despair. When the great foundation of the Word of God is removed from the foundations, great will be the fall. There are really no words to express the devastation.

I have tried to describe this wave of trouble as a Tidal Wave. The reason for the Tidal Wave example was an act of desperation. As I search my mind to try to get the words to emphasize the devastation of losing the Absolute Word, a Tidal Wave was the best example I could find to try to make my point clear. If this Bible watering down continues, we are doomed! Let me explain the reason for the destruction in four simple reasons.

The Four-fold Problem

1. *The Imperatives of Absolute Truth—Thus Saith the Lord!*

Because of the importance of absolute, unmovable truth, we will not be able to withstand the loss of God's Word as absolute unquestionable truth.

> *James 1:6 But let him ask in faith, nothing wavering. For he that wavereth is like a wave of the sea driven with the wind and tossed.*

If there is no Bible authority, there is no absolute, unquestionable truth. We become a people with questions with no answers. Every answer can be questioned and challenged with no resolution no answer. Therefore, we are like waves of the sea with no stability.

2. *The Guards are fallen asleep!*

Because the ones who should be extremely upset, the guards of the Word of God, the ministers, the dedicated Christians, have overlooked the inevitable weakening of the Word by the new translators, paraphrases, the interchanging, diluting of doctrines by restating phrases and word, etc., because the guards have deserted their posts, we are inheriting a tidal wave of destruction. Because the Guards have deserted or have somehow become passive about this issue, there is no one to stop the devastation.

3. *Simple Cause and Effect!*

If the Word becomes weaker by new phrases, wording, paraphrases, etc., the only foundation for absolute truth is weakened and disappears as Christian authority. It already has disappeared as authority in the eyes of the world. Through evolution, lack of Christian heritage being taught and other media promoted assaults, the Word of God has been rejected. But the effects of God's own people's watering of the Word is an irrevocable devastation. Cause and effect is inevitable in Christian circles as well as world circles. The great problem is that God's people refuse to consider that they will be affected by this law of cause and effect.

4. *God's Promised Blessing!*

God has promised to bring fruit by the engrafted Word into our hearts. God has promised to bless all who take His statutes and live them out. But God has also promised to curse all who do not (Deut. 28).

God has also given us His Word filled with changing power.

James 1:21...and receive with meekness the engrafted word, which is able to save your souls.

Psalms 119:9 Wherewithal shall a young man cleanse his way? By taking heed thereto according to Thy word (v. 11) Thy word have I hid in mine heart, that I might not sin against thee.

John 15:3 Now ye are clean through the word which I have spoken unto you.

John 17:17 Sanctify them through thy truth; thy word is truth.

1 Peter 1:22 Seeing ye have purified your souls in obeying the truth through the Spirit unto unfeigned love of the brethren, see that ye love one another with a pure heart fervently.

John 20:31 But these are written, that ye might believe that Jesus is the Christ, the Son of God; and that believing ye might have life through his name.

These are only a few references from God's Word as to its promised power. God will bless His Word, His promises, His truth, etc. God will bless a people who take His word to heart and those who allow the statutes and truths to transform them; He will honor them supremely. Therefore, with God's Word is a power we cannot live without. And a weakened God's Word brings a weakened product. A weakened God's Word breeds weak faith. A weakened God's Word casts doubt on the truth of God's Word.

Remember, the devil, the serpent in the Garden of Eden changed only a few words in God's original statement to cause Eve to fall, and great was the fall of that home. Also during the temptations of Christ, notice the changing of God's promises to try to trip up Jesus. Satan has changed God's Word a little in the past to try to subdue God's servants. I contend that we are now subject to the same assault. Wave Three is so important. Waves One and Two are living examples of what happens when people lose respect for God's absolute authority.

> *Psalm 11:3 If the foundations be destroyed, what can the righteous do?*

Now let's examine the assault against God's Word.

II.   THE MIRACLE OF THE BIBLE

The Bible is a book unlike other books. Its contents have the ability to change a person or to change the destiny of a man's eternal soul. This is a responsibility that no other book has. It contains power over sin, the grave and death.

The Bible is a book like no other book because of its miracle content, yes, but also its miracle consistence, its miracle construction, etc. The Bible was inspired by God and compiled over a period of 4,000 years, from Adam and Eve until John penned the Revelation in A.D. 90 on the island of Patmos. Moses was inspired to write of creation and the fall of man, and the separation from God. John was compelled to write of the eternal destination with God. There were at least 40 different inspired penmen writing the inspired scripture, over a period of at least 2,000 years of penning. At least three continents were involved, and three different languages: Hebrew, Greek and Aramaic. Many different types of writing or literature were involved: poetry, history, drama, law, genealogy, etc. Many different types of personalities: farmers, shepherds, prophets of all sorts, slaves, kings, prisoners, fishermen, religious leaders, etc. All this was against the success of the inspiration, but God inspired a book with miracle results. The consistent pattern is miraculous.

The theme of the Bible was the coming of a Messiah to deliver us from the sin curse placed on us by Adam and Eve. The Lamb was the key to this deliverance. From the lamb that died for Adam and Eve's clothing, to cover their sin, to Cain and Abel's difference over how to worship, and the winner won by a lamb's blood. To God preparing a sacrifice to take the place of Isaac on Mount Moriah, to the Passover Lamb's blood stopping the death angel in Egypt. Then we have the continual sacrifice of lambs through the history of the law with the children of Israel trying to please God with lamb's blood through the atoning lamb once a year to the scapegoat once a year. The picture was cast that a lamb must die for people to be able to face God. Therefore, when John the Baptist said, Behold the Lamb of God, which taketh away the sin of the world," the lamb's blood would be understood. The span of 2,500 years had proclaimed the need of lamb's blood to take away our sin and then came the Lamb sent from God, Jesus.

Take another look: 2,500 years, 40 different authors, from not a people to new people to great people to in-bondage people to scattered people and then an in-gathered people once again in our day. All of this and still consistently reminded, Lamb needed, Lamb delivered. What will we do with the Lamb that God delivered? The Bible informs us of the Lamb, why we need Him, and what He did.

The Bible is a miracle of the past, but is still a miracle in the present. Let me add just one reference to the present-day fulfillments of the holy, inspired Scriptures. Jeremiah 16, the proclamation of the disbursement of the people of Israel to the uttermost parts of the glove, then the re-gathering of them to Jerusalem. Then the big news of the Jews returning in droves from the land of the North. This is our present time miracle. When the walls of Communism came down in the late 1980s and early 1990s the Russian Jews began leaving the Russian provinces (the land north of Jerusalem). Then appeared programming time on national television asking people to help pay for the passage of Russian Jews to return to their homeland. This is the fulfillment of many scriptures but especially Jeremiah 16. Jeremiah's prophecy was written before the Jews were even dispersed.

The Bible also is a book of the future. The Old and new Testaments are filled with prophecies that are fulfilling each day and will be fulfilled in the days ahead. All we need to do is know the truth and we can see it easily. No other book ever in the past or ever in the future ill measure up to this book unless God chooses to all it. Those who reject the scriptures just do not know the facts of the scriptures.

Jesus was prophesied to come of a virgin 600 years before he came. The Christmas story proclaims that he will be called Wonderful, Counseller, The mighty God, the Prince of Peace (Isaiah 9). Let me insert this scripture here because of the importance of making the connection from past to present to future.

Isaiah 9:6-8 For unto us a child is born, unto us a son is given: and the government shall be upon his shoulder: and his name shall be called Wonderful, Counseller, the mighty God, The everlasting Father, the Prince of Peace. Of the increase of his government and peace there shall be no end, upon the throne of David, and upon his kingdom, to order it, and to establish it with judgment and with justice from henceforth even forever. The zeal of

the Lord of hosts will perform this.
The Lord sent a word into Jacob, and
it hath lighted upon Israel.

This prophecy is yet to be completely fulfilled. The Child is born and given to us, but He has yet to be declared the mighty God, etc. He has yet to sit upon David's throne. But this scripture is to come. The future is yet to come. The exciting thing about this is that we will see it; that is, if we have been washed in the blood of the Lamb (Jesus).

Yes, the scripture is a miracle of yesterday, today and tomorrow. But the point I would like to make is the evident consistency. Let me illustrate it this way. If we were to gather 40 different artists together, send them all to a different room and tell them to draw a picture of something that comes to mind, if these artists came out with all different paintings and then put them together and they were the perfect likeness of a man on the cross dying, for the sins of the world this would be a miracle. If 40 sculptures were treated the same way, and out they came with pieces of sculpture that made a perfect statue of Jesus, this would be a miracle. This is really a simulation of what God did. Only His 40 people were not of one sort; they did not live at the same time, nor were they from the same culture, nor were they all writers. I hope you get the point.

The Bible is definitely a miracle. Those who reject this statement simply do not know the facts. Let's move on in our examination of this miracle.

III. THE ORIGIN OF THE BIBLE

The Origin of the Bible is not common knowledge that is possessed by the average Christian. It is knowledge that needs to be known by all especially those from the household of faith.

Language Development

As God created man, He developed language and later compelled people to develop written language. When God wanted to pull man together, He pulled them together by communication. When He decided to separate man, He also used the method of communication, the lack of it (Tower of Babel).

As God desired to reveal Himself to man, He called and commissioned various people to pen His words to them. Sometimes He dictated His words to them. Other times He used the people and their circumstances to give information. But God breathed His message just the same.

The first records of written language (after the Flood of Genesis) were found in Sumeron, not many miles from ancient Ur, where Abraham was from. These writings were pictographs (picture writings) pressed into clay tablets. It is believed by many Bible scholars that this form of communication was necessary after the confusion of languages at the Tower of Babel. A pictorial alphabet. Through initially the most logical way to express ideas, would eventually become ponderous and limiting.

It is believed that Phoenicians invented the first "modern" (post-flood) alphabet, which utilized phonetic sounds in place of pictographs. Writing tools and materials also improved, including the use of goat skins (the original form of "parchment"); however, these were still expensive and inconvenient.

The Egyptians also invented papyrus, or paper. The papyrus plant was cut and lapped together to create a very good writing surface. The sheets of papyrus were glued together to create long sheets for long documents and developed into a scroll.

Scholars differ on the origin and development of the Hebrew alphabet. Some believe that the Hebrew alphabet was first developed after the flood, beginning as a written language of consonants only, eventually adding punctuation marks to provide consistent pronunciation. Over the course of many years, they were able to pen the Old Testament with Hebrew and later a small portion with another language called Aramaic.

Other respected scholars believe that Hebrew may have been the original created language given to Adam and Eve by God. Since we know that Adam and Eve were fully mature and able to communicate with God directly through the spoken language, it is entirely reasonable that they would realize the importance of keeping records for future generations. Noah could easily have preserved these records on the Ark. If this is the case, then it changes the way many people view the origin and development of language.

Several Bible passages refer to the important work of the scribes: Exodus 17:14; Exodus 24:4; Isa. 8:1; Isa 30:8, I cor. 14:37; Jer. 34:6.

The Bible was written in three languages: Hebrew Aramaic and Greek. The Greek language was brought into world acceptance by the Greek empire during Alexander the Great's reign. The Greek language was a very direct and specific language. They not only could tell you they love, but they had a word that described a kind of love they had for you. At the time of Christ's life and throughout the writing of the N.T., the Greek language was used, which provided very precise meanings to words and phrases.

Because the Scriptures span such a range of time from the Old Testament to the New Testament, it is helpful to understand the culture, manners and traditions of individual writers; but the Scriptures themselves tell us much about their origin and meaning.

II Timothy tells us that God breathed the scriptures. Sometimes God burdened men to write about the same experience, such as in the four Gospels. This gave the writings emphasis and also flavor, flavored by the writers' personalities and differences.

The Bible is different than any other book. Why? Because the Bible is old? Yes. Because the Bible tells us of times we need to know about? Yes. Because the Bible tells us about heaven, and etc.? Yes. But the Bible is God's direct Word to man. The Bible is the only Word to man. Therefore, we must guard this Word with our lives! Many have even *given* their lives doing so.

But how do we know which Books are God-breathed? This was the question asked after the death of John the Apostle. After his death there were many books written that weren't inspired. The Church leaders needed a way to determine the true Word of God from simple letters or writings. Therefore, they developed a way to determine God's breathed Word. This takes us to the canon of the scriptures.

The Canon

The earliest parts of the OT were originally inscribed on leather or papyrus in old Hebrew with archaic, prong-shaped letters similar to the script of the earliest recovered Phoenician inscriptions. This archaic writing gradually developed after 400BC. According to conservative scholars, Moses was the first inspired writer, producing the Pentateuch around 1450-1400BC. Malachi, the last of the OT writers, wrote no later than 400 BC.

The canon is a phrase by which the catalog of the authoritative sacred writings is designated. The word for the expression of a driving force, Kanon, originally signified a reed or a standard, norm or rule; especially that which is measured by that standard or norm. Those Books which were measured by the standard or test of divine inspiration and authority and were adjudged to be "God-Breathed" were included in the canon.

Conservatives hold that inspired scripture had the canonical authority from the moment of inspiration by the Spirit of God, independent of formal collection or human recognition. The higher critical view, however is that canonization took extensive time. According to this theory, the Law was first canonized by 44BC. The higher criticism thus assumes that the threefold division of the Hebrew canon is due principally to chronology. It is held that the prophets did not become popular until 300BC., and as a result their writings were collected and canonized within the next century.[xlii]

In the early days of the NT Church many people were writing books, letters and doctrinal statements. Therefore, a lot of care went into filtering the God-breathed Word. Just because a writing was old didn't mean it was God-breathed.

The Apocrypha was a great example for the need of the canon. The Apocrypha was a group of writings, some history, some romance, some stories, etc. Some claimed inspiration and some didn't. But they were all rejected. Why?

- The Jews didn't accept the Apocrypha's old Jewish writings as inspired.
- The Old writings of the Apocrypha (before Christ) were never referred to by Christ.
- Some claimed no divine inspiration.
- Some were full of historical errors.
- Some contained theological errors.

- Some were not consistent with Jesus' teachings or the goals given to us by the OT writers or Jews.

The Apocrypha is valuable information giving us history in areas where we wouldn't have any of the history of Jewish troubled days, for example, Hanukkah, the Jewish holiday, and how it came to be.

But as for inspiration, the Apocrypha is lacking the power of God-breathed inspiration.

The canon was developed to insure the complete and pure Word of God to man. Writings like the Apocrypha and other such writings demanded such a filter. In AD 200 early Church leaders filtered through the existing materials and came forth with the Old and New Testaments, finishing with the Apostle John's Revelation. They felt God was impressing them to close the Bible to other writings. God had informed us from Genesis through Revelation, from beginning through to the eternal forever, therefore completing the story. What more could we need?

The gospel (1 Cor. 15:3-4) was first preached by word of mouth and interpreted in the light of OT history and prophecy. Oral accounts of the life and work of Christ were written down and finally gave way to the inspired Synoptic (agreeing) Gospels sometime before AD70. The need for doctrinal interpretation of Christ's person and work soon became a necessity, accentuated by the need to define Christianity against such errors as legalism and antinomianism (a loose look at morals). The Pauline and other epistles were written to meet this need. The demand for a historical sketch of the development of the church was met by the Book of Acts. Challenges to the Christians to remain true to Christ even until death were met by other writers. Revelation, of course, met the need of future hopes and blessings.

But as these writers were writing, they were being critiqued by the church of the day.

- First, was the writer a bona fide Apostle?
- Second, was content in high order and spiritual harmony with the demands of holy scripture?
- Third, did the Church as a whole receive the book?
- Fourth, was divine inspiration evident? Did the writing breathe the breath of God? Were the words full of power and conviction? Did they speak for God?

Many of the writings of the day were rejected. Without the providential hand of God, the NT canon would never have been correctly created.

There was a group of books that were received as canonized as early as 245AD, by Origen (Early Church leader). All books of the Old and New Testament were canonized using the canon rules to determine the inspired scriptures.

It is important to note that the canonized scriptures were completed before the Catholic Church came to be in 325AD. The NT canon was formed spontaneously, not by the action of church council buy by early Christian leaders not many days after the passing of the Apostle John.

The Bible is such an amazing book! Its completion was by over 40 different writers and covered a time span of 4,000 years in completing. Most of the writers didn't even know each other. The Bible completion covers three different continents. It was written a little at a time, preserved by God Himself, no doubt.

Apart from a few very minor differences, the verdict of the first four centuries has remained the same. During the Reformation of the 13-1500s, the authority of the scriptures was one of the main power sources pushing for reforms and godliness. When people accept His great gift to us as authority, God empowers them as well.

A note of information: It was not until 1546, the Roman Church at the Council of Trent decided to include 11 of the 14 Apocryphal books as part of the canon. This move was totally rejected by the Reformation leaders. Therefore, the Catholic Bible includes them but the English Protestant Bible excludes them.

Origins of the English Bible

Let's discuss the English Bible and how it came to be. There's much that could be said about this great blessing of an English Bible, but for the sake of time I will summarize.

The Bible was, as we have said, originally written in Hebrew, Aramaic and Greek. But due to the takeover of the NT Church by the Roman Empire in 325AD, Constantine being the Emperor, much of the protection and preservation of the scriptures was done by the Roman Catholic Church. The language of Rome because of the influence of Italy had become Latin, therefore, the Catholic Church began to copy the scriptures into Latin. This created a Latin Bible for the Catholic Church. We know this Bible as the Latin Vulgate.

The cost of a Bible was extremely expensive and hard to come by seeing all Bibles were copied by hand and on expensive paper. The Catholic Church progressively turned the communities against them by their overbearing attitudes and demands. The Catholic leadership also began to make decisions about the way people should live and, due to the power of the Church's leaders, evil power seekers soon found their way to the seat of power in the Roman Church. All who opposed the Church, their teachings, etc., were excluded, persecuted and even killed. This created a need to reform the Catholic Church. Many tried to reform the Catholic Church, but were rejected. Therefore, God raised up men who had access to the Latin scriptures and the education to read them.

Up to this point, the Catholic leadership had been successful in stopping any teaching other than their own from gaining acceptance. But God raised up a man named John Wycliffe. He had access to the scriptures because he was a teacher in the Catholic Church. He first tried to reform the Catholic Church but when rejected felt the only hope was to get the Bible into the hands of the common man. The Bible Wycliffe penned was from the Latin Bible (Vulgate), but penned in the language of the common man of the day, English. English had become a prominent language due to the direct competition with church of Rome, the Church of England.

During the rise of English people and the English language, John Wycliffe was burdened by God about the inaccuracy of the teachings of the Roman Church. He penned what we know as the first Bible into English, but from the Latin Vulgate. He was persecuted for his efforts, but God used his work to start the common man thinking for himself. He is credited with planting the seed for the reformation. His time was 1382AD.

Two hundred years later God raised up another, William Tyndale. Tyndale was called to translate the Bible from the OT Hebrew to English and from the NT Greek to English. Tyndale used the Textus Receptus (This phrase will be discussed later). He penned the first version into English from the original manuscripts. His translation was extremely well done, and is almost the forerunner of the KJV. The same manuscripts were used and very little differenced are found between the two.

William Tyndale had to smuggle his Bibles into England due to Catholic persecution. They felt the common man would not be able to handle the teachings of the Bible without their help. But the real truth was that they knew the common man would discover their misinterpretations when reading the Word for himself.

A wonderful blessing took place during Tyndale's life. The printing press was invented by Johannes Gutenberg. This gave Tyndale a power to produce more Bibles than the Catholic Church could confiscate and destroy, therefore, bringing on the Reformation by the power of the Word.

Martin Luther was doing the same as Tyndale at the same time, but he was translating this Bible into German.

Let's list the unfolding of the Bible translations in order. This will give you an idea of how they came to us. As I list them, please remember that many, including Tyndale, were killed for their work, and many suffered great losses to give us this great treasure, the English Bible.

The English Versions of the Bible Translated from the Textus Receptus

Early Anglo-Saxon Versions

Caedmon, by 680, had rendered Bible stories into common speech in poetic paraphrase, according to Bede. Bede (died 735) is credited with a translation of John's Gospel. King Alfred (848-901) had portions of the Bible translated into the vernacular. But until the time of Wycliffe (14th cent.) the Tyndale (16th cent.), the Bible was translated into English only sporadically and piecemeal.

Wycliffe's Version (1382)

This was the first complete translation into English, revised c1400, condemned and burned in 1415. At least 170 MS copies have survived. Its weakness was that it was based on the Latin Vulgate instead of the original Greek.

Tyndale's Translation (1525-35)

Translated from the original Hebrew and Greek, the significance of Tyndale's version lies in its being first in line of translations, so creative and impressive in its style that it formed the backbone of the Authorized King James Version of 1611.

The Coverdale Version (1535)

Miles Coverdale leaned on Tyndale's scholarly work. He supplemented, where it had not been finished, by his own translation from German and Latin. He presented the first complete English Bible in print.

The Thomas Matthew Bible (1537)

Largely a revision of Tyndale by Tyndale's friend John Rogers, it was nevertheless published under the name of Thomas Matthew.

The Taverner's Bible (1539)

A revision by Taverner of the Matthews Bible minus most of the notes and polemic data.

The Great Bible (1539)

The first authorized Bible, called "great" from its size. It was also styled the "Cranmer Bible" because of Archbishop Cranmer's preface to the second edition (1540).

The Geneva Bible (1560)

A revision of the Great Bible.

The Bishops' Bible (1568)

The second Authorized English Bible. It was intended to supersede the Geneva Bible, the Bible of the people, and the Great Bible, the pulpit Bible of the churches. The translation work was done mainly by scholarly bishops.

The Douay Version (1609-10)

The first Roman Catholic Bible in English from the Latin Vulgate, not the Textus Receptus.

The King James Version (1611)

The culmination of these preceding early translations and revisions became the third "authorized" English Bible, sponsored by James I of England. It employed the chapter divisions of Stephen Langton, archbishop of Canterbury in the 13th century, and the verse divisions of Robert

Estienne (1551).   The version reigned supreme from 1611 to 1881.

These are the translations of the Textus Receptus. Then something happened. We will discuss what happened a little later but, for now, please notice the shift in translations. These next translations were rejected by all conservatives at the time of their release. Why? Manuscripts! A completely different set of manuscripts began to be used to translate the new translations. Let's list them and then we will discuss this manuscript dilemma.

The Bibles Translated from the Nestle Aland Manuscripts

The Revised Version (1881-85)

The Unger's Bible Handbook describes this new version in this way. "A version of the King James Version based on literal translation of the Greek and Hebrew texts by sixty-five English scholars." But what they do not say is that the manuscripts were completely changed for this Bible. A new set of manuscripts was used. This version was also rejected by all conservatives at the time of its translation.

The American Standard Version (1901)

An American edition of the Revised Version of 1885, including preferred readings and format changes, by a group of American scholars under the direction of William H. Green of Princeton Seminary.

The Revised Standard Version of the Bible (1952)

New Testament (1946). Authorized by the National Council of Churches of Christ in the U.S.A., widely used by denominations in that group and many not in its membership. Although this version has many excellencies, it is weak and obscure in its translation of certain key OT messianic passages.

The New English Bible: New Testament (1961)

A completely new translation by English scholars under the direction of C.H. Dodd of Cambridge. It is aimed at rendering the original Greek into idiomatic English, free from archaisms and from transient modernisms. It has enjoyed an enthusiastic reception in the U.S., but not without question by many evangelicals.

Modern Speech Translation

The Twentieth Century New Testament (1898-1901)

By an anonymous group of scholars, revised in 1904.

The New Testament in Modern Speech (1903)

By Richard F. Weymouth, revised twice by others.

The New Testament: An American Translation (1923)

By Edgar J. Goodspeed, in American colloquial language.

The New Testament: The Berkeley Version in Modern English (1945)

By Gerrit Verkuyl. The Old Testament was completed in 1959 by a group of conservative scholars.

The New Testament in Plain English (1952)

By Charles Kingsley Williams.

An Expanded Translation of the New Testament (1956-59)

By Kenneth S. Wuest.

The New Testament in Modern English (1958)

By J. B. Phillips. Four previously published translations beginning with letters to Young Churches (1947), were published as a single volume New Testament in 1958.

The Amplified Bible: The New Testament (1958)

Old Testament (1962-64). The complete Bible was published in one volume in 1965. An attempt to add clarifying shades of meaning to the single-word English equivalents of key Hebrew and Greek words.

The New American Standard Bible: New Testament (1960-63)

A revision of the American Standard Version (1901) by a group of conservative scholars.

Living Letters: The Paraphrased Epistles (1962)
Living Prophecies: The Minor Prophets Paraphrased with Daniel and Revelation (1965)

By Kenneth N. Taylor.

The New Testament in the Language of Today (1963)

By William F. Beck.[xliii]

There are many other modern-day translations that I will not even mention. They are continually coming off the presses. But all are translated from the manuscripts of the new versions, called the Nestle-Aland Manuscripts. The question is a big, "Why?" Why, after 1,500 years, the canon of the scriptures and the blood, sweat and tears that brought us the Bible? Why the change in manuscripts? The early scholars and canon representatives felt the manuscripts they were using were the closest and the best. What could convince the scriptural guards to change such a solid foundation?

Let's move into the manuscript section and explain.

IV.   THE MANUSCRIPTS OF THE BIBLE

There are over 5,000 copies of manuscripts known in the world today—5,366 to be exact. These are not total Bibles but sections of scriptures that have been found and gathered.

When the Bible was being canonized, the early scholars gathered all the copies they could find and then began a process of the canon and also a process of deciding which of the 5,366 copies could be trusted. The 5,366 were copies. The originals were worn away due to their heavy use and travel, and also due to the type of paper and materials used. But these 5,366 were carefully copied by the godly men of the day. The God who brought us the Bible is able to empower these men to carefully bring us the scriptures.

These canon scholars were filtering these manuscripts and found that there were about 20% of these manuscripts that did not agree with each other nor did they agree with the other 80% was compiled and used to translate the Bible from 245AD until 1881. This manuscript is known by a few names. The *True Text* it was called. The *Majority Manuscript* it was called. The *Traditional Manuscript* it was called. The *Byzantine Text* it was called. But we know this text by its more familiar name, The *Textus Receptus*. Let me give you just a brief description of why these names were used.

1. *The True Text:* Called the true text because the forefathers of the early church studied the manuscripts and believed it to be the true text out of all found

2. *The Majority Text:* Called the Majority Text because of all the manuscripts used in completing the manuscripts called the true text. There was a vast majority of agreement in these manuscripts and taking into consideration the many people who handled them, that's a miracle in itself. 80-90% agreement with only small areas of non-agreement.

3. *The Traditional Text:* Called the Traditional Text because of the years and years of acceptance. This text was handed down from generation to generation as the traditional, accepted text of our church fathers.

4. *The Byzantine Text:* Called the Byzantine Text because of the area in which it originated. In AD 330 Constantine, the Roman Emperor who adopted Christianity, moved the capital of Rome to Constantinople, a new city built on the remains of the Byzantine Empire. Therefore, this was a time of peace and the beginning of public worship. This was the beginning of the Catholic Church. This is where the Majority Text seemed to bloom and have its roots.

5. *The Textus Receptus:* Called the Textus Receptus because it was the manuscript primarily developed in the early 1500's by Erasmus for monastery study. This Textus Receptus differed from the Traditional Text only four times.

These five different names were primarily the same text with only a few exceptions. The time span of AD 245-1500 brought name changes but primarily the same accepted text. These manuscripts are also referred to as *Eastern Manuscripts.* This was the accepted text by all the founding fathers of the NT Church from AD 200-1800. This was the translating text until 1881AD.

Question: What happened to the 20% manuscripts that were discarded as unacceptable?

Answer: They were put away and labeled "flawed" because of their lack of harmony, agreement and contextual accuracy. They were also Western in their origin, meaning they came from the Alexandria, Egypt area. They were also written in a different type of Greek, influenced by the Alexandrian Greek. Therefore, for many reasons they were discarded.

But here is where the tidal wave to come began to mount a potential problem.

The time was 1870. The place was Oxford University in England. The event, a group of Anglican-Catholic clergymen decided to revise the King James Version of the Bible. There were two predominant men at Oxford who influenced the revision more than anyone else, Doctor Brooke Foss Westcott and Fenton John Anthony Hort. Westcott later became bishop of Durham, the fourth-ranking bishop of the Anglican Church in England. At the time of his graduation, Westcott had feared that he would have to sign belief in the 39 Articles of Faith of the Anglican Church, for he no longer assented to them. Both men were believers in Mary worship and, without hesitation, I can say they left a lot to be desired in the Christian or godly category. Hort was found later to have written letters explaining his desire to discredit the KJV and discourage the Protestant movement. I know these are strong words, but I wouldn't be saying them if there weren't a lot of evidence that proclaimed them true.

Hort and Westcott led a successful effort to retrieve the 20% disagreeing manuscripts from the rejected file and replace the traditionally accepted Text. This is hard for me to believe. How two men could so captivate the Christian leadership into receiving such a change is beyond understanding. But let's think for a moment of Darwin. Darwin's theory of evolution makes no scientific sense and continually has been found to be foolishness, but still is accepted and taught by the very people who should be shouting its flaws. Again, one woman successfully persuaded the United States government to take the valuable Scriptures and prayer away from our children, and even though they are killing each other without conscience and purpose, still they are left in need—absent is God's Word. Therefore, we can understand how this could be. But just as Ken

Ham, Henry Morris and others are shouting at Darwin's destructive foundation, and David Barton, Peter Marshall and others are shouting about the Christless history dilemma, I am trying to help the world see the destruction coming in our churches because of the watering down of God's Word. I can already see the evidence of it.

Yes, Hort and Westcott, with their Oxford influence, led a surprising revolution of replacing of the accepted translation text. They replaced the *Traditional Text* with the *Minority Text*. How? By saying they had found two manuscripts that were *thought* to be older than any existing manuscripts at the time. The two manuscripts were older but non-agreeing. They were also Western Texts, written and aligned with the 20% minority, discarded manuscripts. Somehow Hort and Westcott surprised themselves and were able to convince the group desiring to revise the KJV to use these manuscripts previously rejected by all because of the two manuscripts found that were supposed to be the oldest—even if they disagreed with the majority of the manuscripts. This did not happen without opposition. There was opposition, but down through the years their minority manuscript has become the accepted without the Christians even realizing the change or that there is a problem. From 1881, The Revised Version, each new Bible is translated from the rejected manuscripts. Some call them *Aleph and B* manuscripts, but most Christians today know them as the *Nestle-Aland* manuscript.

Therefore, when a young minister goes off to Bible college to be schooled in Greek, he is sold a Nestle-Aland manuscript to translate, and he is never told any different. He simply accepts it as the best and translates away. The problem comes when he tries to line the Nestle-Aland Manuscript up beside the KJV. They are not exactly the same so he simply says that the KJV is not with the original. But the truth is that he has been sold a manuscript that is not the one used to translate the KJV.

Therefore, we have a manuscript dilemma. There is much to read and study in the change, and there are many who are trying to inform people as I. But I wanted to keep it simple for you. If you want further information, and I hope you do, see the bibliography. But let me just insert a few statements from very well-versed men so you will not think that I am alone in my perception of this dilemma.

Wilbur Pickering, author of *The Identity of the New Testament Text* and a recipient of a TH.M. in Greek Exegesis from Dallas Theological Seminary and M.A. and Ph.D. in Linguistics from the University of Toronto says:

> *The distressing realization is forced upon us that the progress of the past hundred years has been precisely in—the wrong direction— our modern versions and critical texts are found to differ from the Original in some six thousand places, many of them being serious differences...(They) are several times farther removed from the originals than are the A.V. (Authorized*

Version) and TR (Textus Receptus) (KJV and its foundation, the Greek Textus Receptus).How could such a calamity have come upon us...much of the work that has been done is flawed. [xliv]

Dean John Burgon, the scholar who has collated the most early New Testament witnesses (87,000), says of the changes in one of the 'new' versions and Greek text:

Ordinary readers...will of course assume that the changes result from the reviser's skill in translating—advances which have been made in the study of Greek. It was found that they had erred through defective scholarship to an extent and with a frequency, which to me is simply inexplicable...Anything more unscientific...can scarcely be conceived, but it has prevailed for fifty years. We regret to discover that...their work is disfigured throughout by changes which convict a majority of their body alike of an imperfect acquaintance with the Greek language. [xlv]

Edward F. Hills, author of *The King James Version Defended* and graduate of Yale University, Westminster Theological Seminary and recipient of a Ph.D. from Harvard and a TH.M. from Columbia University say:

Modern speech Bibles are unscholarly. [xlvi]

The late E.W. Colwell, past president of the University of Chicago and the premier North American New Testament Greek scholar, authored scores of books, such as *Studies in Methodology in Textual Criticism of the New Testament.* He confesses his "Change of heart" concerning the reliability of readings in the new versions:

> *(S)cholars now believe that most errors were made deliberately...the variant readings in the New Testament were created for theological or dogmatic reasons. Most of the manuals now in print (including mine!) will tell you that these variations were the fruit of careless treatment...The reverse is the case.* [xlvii]

Zane Hodges, professor of New Testament Literature and Exegesis at Dallas Theological Seminary and co-editor of a Greek New Testament refers to new versions as:

> *Monstrously unscientific, if not dangerously obscurantist. The average well-taught Bible-believing Christian has often heard the King James Version corrected on the basis of 'better manuscripts' or 'older authorities'...Lacking any kind of technical training in this area, the average believer probably has*

accepted such explanations from an individual he regards as qualified to give them.[xlviii]

William Palmer, scholar and author of *Narrative of Events the Tracts*, says:

> *(O)rdinary Christians have little idea (concerning the new Greek text)...it rests in many cases on quotations which are not genuine...on passages which when collated with the original, are proved to be wholly in efficacious as proof.*[xlix]

These are a few of the scholarly men who are trying to expose this tidal wave but seem to find people's ears closed. But I hope your ears are open an, like me, you will become vocal about this coming wave of destruction.

I hope you understand that the *Traditional Text* was replaced by a minority text—it took years but now is accepted as the best. Therefore, all new translations are from the *Minority Text*. This is a simple explanation of the manuscript dilemma or change. But I do want to say a little about the men behind the manuscripts.

The Men Behind the Manuscripts

In the section I would like to identify the two families behind the manuscripts. Family one is the Traditional Text family, the Textus Receptus. But for the sake of comparison let's use the name sometimes used to refer to this set of manuscripts, the Majority Text. Family two is the Nestle-Aland, Hort-Westcott, sometimes referred to as the Minority Text. So we have a Majority Text and a Minority Text. Let's refer to the men behind these texts as the family of the text, or manuscripts.

The Majority Text Family

Let's start with the Majority Text Family. AD 100-150 Didache, Diognelus, Justin Martyr—150-200 Athenagouis, Hegesippus-Irenaeus—200-250 Clement, Tertullian, Origen, Novatian, Clementinus, Hippolytus—250-300 Gregory of Thaumatugus, Cyprian, Dionysius, Achelaus – 300-400 Athanasius, Macarius Magnus, Eusebius, Hilary, Didymus, Brasi, Titus of Bostra, Cyril of Jerusalem, Gregory of Nyssa. Apostolic Canons and Constitutions: Epiphanius, Ambrose. These are the men involved in the canon and the creating of the Majority manuscript as well as the discarding of the Minority manuscript.

Then we may jump forward into the future to 1300-1500 where we find John Wycliffe, William Tyndale, Huss, and Luther, etc., giving their lives for the Word. They are a vital part of the Majority manuscript family.

But what about the King James Version translators. Let's take just a minute and examine the translators.

King James, King of England in the early 1600s, decided he wanted a Bible for the common man. He also wanted a Bible translated with the best scholars possible in translation. A diligent search was commissioned for men who had taken pains in their private study of the Scriptures, so as to secure a qualified team of translators. In July of 1607 James had made public his personal selection of fifty-four of the kingdom's brightest intellects. By the time the project was formally begun in 1607, the number of participants had been reduced by seven.

The revisers were divided into six companies and assigned to be at three locations. In the famed Jerusalem Chamber at Westminster, ten men under the direction of the erudite Lancelot Andrews translated Genesis through II Kings, which William Barlow chaired a second company of seven to work with Romans through Jude. At Oxford, John Harding led another seven to labor on Isaiah through Malachi, with a Greek committee of eight completing the Gospels, Acts and Revelation under the chairmanship of Thomas Davis.

The Cambridge groups toiled exclusively from Hebrew: Edward Lively's team of eight rendering I Chronicles through Song of Solomon, which the remaining seven men worked with John Bois to translate the Apocrypha. The Church of Jesus Christ will be forever indebted to the following team of Spirit-filled scholars for giving us our King James Bible. Let's name them.

Dr. Richard Clark, fellow of Christ's Coll., Camb. (Westminster)

Dr. John Layfield, fellow of Trin Coll., Camb (Westminster)

Dr. Robert Teigh, archdeacon of Middlesex (Westminster)

Mr. Francis Burleight, Pemb Hall, Cam. D.D. (Westminster)

Mr. Geoffrey King, fellow of King's Coll., Camb. (Westminster)

Mr. Thompson, Clare Hall, Camb. (Westminster)

Mr. William Bedwell, St. John's Coll., Camb (Westminster)

Mr. Edward Lively, fellow of Trin. Coll. (Cambridge)

Mr. John Richardson, aftwds Master of Trin. Coll. (Cambridge)

Mr. Laurence Chatterton, master of Emm. College (Cambridge)

Mr. Francis Dillingham, fellow of Christ's Coll. (Cambridge)

Mr. Thomas Harrison, vice-master of Trin. Coll. (Cambridge)

Mr. Roger Andrewes, aftwds master of Jesus Coll. (Cambridge)

Mr. Robert Spalding, fellow of St. John's (Cambridge)

Mr. Andrew Byng, fellow of St. Peter's Coll. (Cambridge)

Dr. John Harding, pres. Of Magd. Coll. (Oxford)

Dr. John Reynolds, pres. Of Corpus Christi Coll. (Oxford)

Dr. Thomas Holland, aftwds rector of Ex. Coll. (Oxford)

Dr. Richard Kilbye, rector of Lincoln Coll. (Oxford)

Dr. Miles Smith, Brasenose Coll. (Oxford)

Dr. Richard Fairclough, fellow of New Coll. (Oxford)

Dr. John Duport, master of Jesus Coll. (Cambridge)

Dr. William Branthwait, master of Caius Coll. (Cambridge)

Dr. Jeremiah Radcliffe, fellos of Trin. Coll. (Cambridge)

Dr. Samuel Ward, aftwds master of Sid. Coll. (Cambridge)

Mr. Andrew Downes, fellow of St. John's Coll. (Cambridge)

Mr. John Bois, fellow of St. John's Coll. (Cambridge)

Mr. Robert Warde, fellow of King's Coll. (Cambridge)

Dr. Thomas Ravis, dean of Christ Church (Oxford)

Dr. George Abbot, dean of Winchester (Oxford)

Dr. Richard Eedes, dean of Worcester (Oxford)

Dr. Giles Thompson, dean of Windsor (Oxford

Mr. (Sir Henry) Saville, provost of Eton. (Oxford)

Dr. John Perin, fellow of St. John's Coll. (Oxford)

Dr. Ravens, (fellow of St. John's Coll.) (Oxford)

Dr. John Harmer, fellow of New. Coll. (Oxford)

Dr. William Barlow, dean of Chester (Westminster)

Dr. William Hutchinson, archdeacon of St. Albans (Westminster)
Dr. John Spencer, pres. Of Corp. Chr. Coll. Ox. (Westminster)
Dr. Roger Fenton, fellow of Pemb Hall, Cam. (Westminster)
Mr. Michael Rabbett, Trin. Coll., Camb. (Westminster)
Mr. Thomas Sanderson, Balliol Coll., Oxford, D.D. (Westminster)
Mr. William Dakins, fellow of Trin. Coll., Camb. (Westminster)

James had requested that the translation would have the aid of all principal learned men within the kingdom of England. The excellent biographical sketches contained in Alexander McClure's *The Translators Revisited* and *The Men Behind the King James Version* by Gustavus S. Pain confirm that this royal wish was more than realized. Some have talked about this group in a negative way, but where are the modern scholars who can compete with the men of the KJV committee?

Dr. Sam Gipp writes:

"The men on the translation committee of the King James Bible were, without dispute, the most learned men of their day, vastly qualified for the job they undertook. They were overall both academically qualified by their cumulative knowledge and spiritually qualified by their exemplary lives. Among their

company were men who, academically, took a month's vacation and used the time to learn and master an entirely foreign language; wrote a Persian dictionary; invented a specialized mathematical ruler; one was an architect; mastered oriental languages; publicly debated Greek; tutored Queen Elizabeth in Greek and mathematics; and of one if was said, "Hebrew he had at his fingertips."

When John Bois was only five years old, his father taught him to read Hebrew. By the time he was six, he could not only write the same, but in a fair and elegant character. At age fifteen, he was already a student at St. John's College, Cambridge, where he was renowned for corresponding with his superiors in Greek.

Though engulfed with his studies, Bois made time for his mother, frequently hiking some twenty miles just to have breakfast with her. He would read as he walked. His devouring of over sixty grammars made him one of the most popular Greek professors at Cambridge with students attending his voluntary lectures as early as four a.m. Afterwards, he would remain with his books until eight p.m., studying on his feet and resting only on his knees. Of the man destined to become the committee's final editor, McClure said, "He was so familiar with the Greek Testament that he could, at any time, turn to any word that it contained. The secret to such a consecrated life can be summed up in the translator's own words.

He said, "There has not been a day for these many years in which I have not meditated at least once upon my death."

It was said of Miles Smith that he was "a very walking library." For an attitude that was, "covetous of nothing but books," his was the privilege of writing the new Bible's preface. George Abbot entered Oxford at fourteen years of age and later became the Archbishop of Canterbury. Andrew Downes was described by Milton as the "chief of learned men in England." The literary accomplishments of Thomas Ravis (eventual successor to Bancroft, Bishop of London) at Oxford were representative of translators as a whole: Bachelor of Art, 1578; Master of Arts, 1581; Bachelor of Divinity, 1589; Doctor of Divinity, 1595.

Having become a fellow at Corpus Christi College at age 17, Dr. John Rainolds was known as "a living library, a third university." Anthony Woods says that he was "most prodigiously seen in all kinds of learning; most excellent in all tongues." As well as "apodigy in reading, famous in doctrine, and the very treasure of erudition." In the providence of God, however, the good Dr. Rainolds did not live through the project he initiated. When urged by his friends to ease up his strenuous schedule, he replied, "Non propeter vitam, vevendi perdere causas," "for the sake of life, he would not lose the very end of living." Expiring on the 21st of May, 1607, he was replaced as president of Corpus Christi College by another translator, John Spencer, who himself had been on the Greek faculty since nineteen years of age.

It should be noted that these amazing scholars were not just a bunch of dry theologians, but accomplished preachers and balanced Christians as well. Although proficient in Latin, Greek, Hebrew, Chaldee, Arabic and several Ethiopic tongues, it was said of Richard Brett that, "He was a most vigilant pastor, a diligent preacher of God's Word, a liberal benefactor to the poor, a faithful friend, and a good neighbor."

Thomas Fuller says of Lancelot Andrews that "he was an inimitable preacher in his way; and such plagiarists as have stolen his sermons could never steal his preaching, and could make nothing of that, whereof he made all things as he desired."

One of the eight translators whose responsibilities included the chapter on life's setting sun in Ecclesiastes 12 was Lawrence Chaderton, who himself lived to the ripe old age of one hundred and three. Described as a "grave, pious and excellent preacher," McClure relates an incredible account of his pulpit power: "It is stated on high authority, that while our aged saint was visiting some friends in his native country of Lancashire, he was invited to preach. Having addressed his audience for two full hours by the glass, he paused and said, 'I will no longer trespass on your patience.' And now comes the marvel; for the whole congregation cried out with one consent, - 'For God's sake, go on, go on!' He accordingly, proceeded much longer, to their satisfaction and delight." Not only are congregations such as these conspicuously absent in our present lukewarm age, but the fiery preaching which they heard is absent as well. Citing a sermon excerpt from Richard Kilby of the Oxford team (Old Testament), Paine records, "Consider well what He hath done for you. He made you at the first like Himself, in wisdom and holiness, and when you were by sin made like the devil, and must therefore have been condemned to hell's torments, God sent His only Son, who, taking unto Him a body and soul, was a man and suffered great wrong and shameful death, to secure your pardon, and to put you out of the devil's bondage, that ye might be renewed to the likeness of God...to the end ye might be fit to keep company with all the joys of heaven."

First and foremost, the translators were men of pronounced godliness and spiritual power. It was said that when Lancelot Andrews was near, King James "desisted from mirth and frivolity in his presence."

The unusual diary entries of twenty-seven-year-old Samuel Ward, youngest of the translators, speaks volumes, condemning himself in the second person, he wrote:

> *May 13, 1595, "Thy wandering regard in chapel at prayer time..."*
> *May 17th, "Thy gluttony the night before."*
> *May 23rd, "My sleeping without remembering my last thought, which should have been of God."*
> *May 26th, "Thy dullness this day in hearing God's Word."*

Writing on the subject of divinity, Rainolds declared: "With that divinity, the knowledge of God, is the water of life, the vessel must be cleansed that shall have God's Holy Spirit not only a guest but also a continual dweller within. God forbid that you should think divinity consists of words, as a wood doth of trees. Divinity without godliness doth but condemn consciences against the day of vengeance, and provide the wrath of the might Lord, and make more inexcusable before the seat of judgment. True divinity cannot be learned unless we frame our hearts and minds wholly to it."

Therefore, I wanted you to get a good idea the type of people behind the King James and the manuscript dilemma.

Now let's consider the family behind the Minority Text.

The Minority Text Family

The Minority Text family is not as long nor is it as colorful as the Majority text. The Minority Text has only been used since 1881—until then the text was simply on the scrap heap. But there is a story behind it. We have already covered the retrieving of the minority manuscript earlier in the manuscript chapter. Now let's discuss the characters behind the retrieving of this manuscript.

The two main men who need to be discussed here are the two primarily responsible for the manuscript change. These two men worked to promote a new Greek text to replace the KJV text. Cloaked in what was seen as scholarship, they introduced and pushed their version of the Greek text. At the time of their promotion, the men of scholarship on the scene wouldn't have anything to do with these men or their manuscripts. But they attracted a few in the future who followed them and considered them great scholars and began to push their theories and new Greek text.

These two men originated and put together these new manuscripts. They are a big part of weakening the solid view of the Bible. They are compelling a new generation to have doubts and their confidence hampered.

Wilburn N. Pickering, author of *The Identity of the New Testament Text* (Nashville: Thomas Nelson, publishers, 1980, pp. 38, 42, 96, 90) reveals:

> *The dead hand of Fenton John Anthony Hort lies heavy upon us (Colwell). The two most popular manual editors of the Greek text today. Nestle-Aland and UBS (United Bible Society) really vary little from the W-H text. Why is this? Westcott and Hort are generally credited with having finished the death blow (to the KJV and the Greek text) which was used for the previous 1880 years. Early scholarship has tended to recognize Hort's mistakes. The W-H critical theory is erroneous at every point. Our conclusions concerning*

the theory apply also to any Greek text constructed on the basis of it (Nestle-Aland, UBS, etc.) as well as those versions based on such texts (NIV, NASB, Good News for Modern Man, etc.).

H.C. Hoskier's *A Full Account and Collation of the Greek Cursive Codes Evangelism 604* (London: David Nutt 1870), Introduction pp and *Codex B and Its Allies – A Study and an Indictment* (2 vols. London: Bernard Quaritch Ltd. 1943) notes:

The text printed by Westcott and Hort has been accepted as the true text, and grammars, work on the synoptic problem, works on higher criticism, and others have been grounded on this text. These foundations must be demolished.

Alfred Martin, former Vice President of Moody Bible Institute in Chicago, says: "Many people, even today, who have no idea what the Wescott-Hort theory is, accept the labors of those two scholars without question. An amazing spectacle presents itself. Many of the textbooks, books of Bible interpretation, and innumerable secondary works go on repeating the Westcott and Hort dicta although the foundations have been seriously shaken, even in the opinion of former Hortians.

Since Westcott and Hort are the basis of the foundation for the new translators, this chapter will document what objective secular history says when inspecting these footings. The Voice of Westcott and Hort beckoning from the biographies will further warn what has gone on underground.

In the Life of Westcott you will be surprised to know that the Cambridge undergraduate organized a club and chose for its name, Hermes.[1] The designation is derived from "the god of magic, occult wisdom, the conduction of souls to Hades, lord of death, cunning and trickery."

We do not understand why a Bible student would be the founder of such a club but Westcott and Hort met weekly for three years from 1845-1848, discussing such topics as the Funeral Ceremonies of the Romans, the Eleatic Schools of Philosophers, the Mythology of Homeric Poems, the Theramines and numerous undisclosed subjects.[li]

Westcott and Hort did not stop with their Hermes club, but went on to engage in spiritualism and to organize a society called the Ghostly Guild. The Ghostly Guild was a group of people who were interested primarily in psychic phenomena, ghost investigation and that type of phenomena. Hort and Westcott were very involved in strange spiritual research that was very questionable then and is more so now.

Hort was documented to have desired to rid the world of the KJV foundation text. He said that conservative evangelicals were dangerous, perverted, unsound and confused. Hort's mother was an evangelical Christian. Her influence must have pressed him to examine Christianity. Hort's biography states that he outgrew the evangelical teaching which he came to regard as fanaticism and perverted.

> In Hort's biography, his mother said this about her son: Her religious feelings were deep and strong. His mother was...an adherent of the evangelical school and she was to a certain degree, hampered by it. She was unable to enter into his theological views which to her generation seemed a desertion of the ancient way; thus pathetically enough, there came to be a barrier between mother and son. The close intercourse on subjects which lay nearest to the hearts of each was broken. Concerning her different point of view...he had to recognize that the point of view was different. She studied and knew her Bible well.[lii]

His mother wrote to him, pleading that he would not be missing from the many mansions of our Heavenly Father's house. She said, "My darling, how happy it will be if we all meet there, no one missing of all our household." [liii]

As Hort's career progressed, he retained his distaste for Evangelicals who held tenaciously to the articles of the Christian faith. Hort writes to Lightfoot, mocking an Evangelical bishop.

Claughton's fierce denunciation of everyone show questions an article of the Christian faith as an enemy of God and holiness "(There are) serious differences between us on the subject of authority, and especially the authority of the Bible." [liv]

Fourteen years after his instigation of the Ghostly Guide with Westcott and Benson, Hort writes, "During the last 15 years my thoughts and pursuits have grown and expanded but not considerably changed. In theology itself I am obligated to hold a peculiar position, belonging to no party, yet having important agreements and sympathies with all. I perhaps have more in

*common with the liberal party than
with others. I look upon freedom and
a wide toleration as indispensable."*
lv

Well, what about these two men, the fathers
of the new translation texts? A chaser of ghosts,
a detestor of evangelicals, Hort calls himself a
liberal. But the most staggering of all is the letter
of Hort's mother encouraging her son not to miss
heaven.

> *The two men most responsible
> for modern alterations in the New
> Testament text were B.F. Westcott
> and F.J.A. Hort, whose Greek New
> Testament text has largely replaced
> the traditional Textus Receptus in
> modern seminaries, especially as
> revised and updated by the German
> Eberhard Nestle and Kurt Aland. All
> of these men were evolutionists.
> Furthermore, Westcott and Hort,
> although they were Anglican officials
> and nominally orthodox in theology,
> both denied biblical inerrancy,
> promoted racism, and even dabbled in
> spiritualism. Nestle and Aland, like
> Kittel, were German theological
> liberals.*

> *Westcott and Hort were also
> the most influential members of the
> English revision committee that
> produced the English Revised Version
> of the Bible, published in 1881. The*

corresponding American revision committee which developed the American Standard Version of 1901 was headed by another liberal evolutionist, Philip Schaff. Most new versions since that time have favored the same manuscripts and assumptions as did those 19th revisers. Schaff was twice tried for heresy by his denomination and taught at the very liberal Union Seminary. As chairman of the revision committee, Schaff not only was greatly influenced by Westcott and Hort, but also by the Unitarians Ezra Abbot and Joseph Thayer of Harvard, as well as other liberals whom he placed on the committee.

Furthermore, the changes adopted by the Westcott-Hort (or Nestle-Aland) Greek texts were predominantly based on two old Greek manuscripts, the Sinaitucus and Vaticanus texts, which were rediscovered and rescued from long (and well-deserved) obscurity in the 19th century. Since these are both supposedly older than the more than 5,000 manuscripts that general support the Textus Receptus, they were accepted as "better." This was in spite of the fact that they frequently disagreed with each other as well as with the Textus Receptus and also contained many serious and obvious omissions. The Vatican manuscript for example, leaves out most of Genesis as well as all of Revelation, in addition to the pastoral epistles of Paul, 33 Psalms, and over a third of Hebrews.

The fact that these two manuscripts are older obviously does not prove they are better. More likely it indicates that they were set aside and not used because of their numerous gross errors. Thus they would naturally last longer than the good manuscripts which were being used regularly and thus wore out sooner.

The Sinaitic manuscript was reportedly rescued from a wastebasket in a monastery on Mount Sinai by another German evolutionist theologian, Freidrich Tischendorf. The Orthodox monks evidently had long since decided that the numerous omissions and alterations in the manuscript had rendered it useless and had stored it away in some closet where it had remained unused for centuries. Et Tischendorf promoted it widely and vigorously as representing a more accurate text than the thousands of manuscripts supporting the traditional Byzantine text.

A similar mystery applies to the famous Vatican manuscript, which had been kept in seclusion in the Vatican Library since 1480 or earlier, though no one seemingly knows for sure when it was originally written or how it was acquired by the Vatican.

Tischendorf learned of its existence and again was instrumental I promoting its antiquity and superiority to the Textus Receptus. [lvi]

Prominent Modern Translations

Let's discuss just briefly the three most prominently used translations of our day from the minority manuscripts, the NIV, NASB and NKJV.

NIV-New International Version

Translated by interdenominational translators, therefore, the multidenominational committee was influenced by their beliefs. Also, they were hard pressed when dealing with denominational differences. Minority Manuscripts were used.

NASB-New American Standard Bible

The chairman of the committee was Philip Schaff. Henry Morris calls him a liberal evolutionist. Also Minority Manuscripts were used, of course.

This is using the King James name, but the translators used a combination approach in translation. They used the Minority and the Majority manuscripts. Some of the translators who worked on the NIV also worked on the NKJV. The translators examined both sets of manuscripts and then decided which one they would use. They seem to be trying to make everyone happy and have the best of both worlds. Some would say that this is good. But what it does is gives a translator the power to choose which text to translate from, rather than just giving you God's Word. Therefore, we still have the minority manuscripts' influence, the Hort-Westcott shadow, etc.

If you would like more information on the NKJV, write to Trinitarian Bible Society, (USA), 1710 Richmond N.W., Grand Rapids, Michigan 49504, or call (616) 453-2892.

There is much more that could be said about the two men Hort and Westcott and the translation dilemma. The bibliography will give you much to read for yourself, if my small summary is not enough to let you know what kind of men were behind the new manuscripts, or the new versions. But I think there is really no question that we have much to be concerned about. It is also easy to figure why the early 1900 religious leadership so rejected these new translations from these Hort-Westcott Manuscripts.

I want you to know that their questionable walk with God was and is well-known among those who inquire. The questionable walk is well-known, but not talked about for some unknown reason. But the ones who I have talked to (in the know about any of what I have told you) just don't seem to think Hort and Westcott's questionable Christian character is important. How do you explain that?

Personally, I cannot see any reason why solid-foundation Christians would accept these flawed manuscripts or the Bibles that sprang from them. Hort and Westcott were lacking much, simply put. They were anti-conservative, and anti-evangelical. They were pro-liberal, pro-spiritualists, and pro-problem

Which family do you trust, the Minority family of Westcott-Hort, Nestle-Aland, Philip Schaff, etc., or the Textus Receptus, Majority Manuscript family of Origen, Wycliffe, Tyndale, D.L. Moody, George Whitefield, the King James translators, etc.?

V. THE WEAKENED WORD AND WORSENING WORLD

It is extremely hard to get people to understand the weakening taking place in the new translations. Whether by manuscripts, money or cultural acceptance, whatever the reason, the weakening is still taking place.

I want to take just a small area and show a few of the very important examples of the weakening wave. This will be just a few examples, but if you want more, consult the bibliography in the rear of this book.

Let me challenge you to open your new versions and check the accuracy and truth of what is about to be said, and allow God to show you that we are all a part of the prophetic deception Satan has put together. And, just like a lot of others, we didn't realize the pattern and the powerful potential of the new versions.

I am not trying to dictate to you what version to read. My purpose is to expose truth and help all to be alert to the serpent's head as he slowly slides into our churches and homes. The decision you make is up to you. I hope you will allow God to give you the knowledge, wisdom and courage to do God's will as a good soldier of Jesus Christ.

AS we have discussed the manuscript changes, the men who brought about the change and their character, you can see the fruit that has already begun to come forth as a result of the changes. The most evident fruit is the weak pulpits that have come forth from the new version preachers.

The translations of the Bible and the word altering is not only an old trick used by Satan, but a very effective one. It is also very important to him to change the Bible, because the Bible is God's communication channel to man. Man must not be confused concerning the way to receive the Redeemer. This is the foundation on which all joy of life depends, and eternal life as well. We must make connection with God through His Son. We must become cleansed by the blood. We must not lose any of the truth God has, through His blood, given us. The redemption, regeneration and future of man depends totally on this truth. The power of the blood is to cleanse man of sin and give him a clear conscience. Do you see the power of the Word and the great gift of God? In light of the importance of the Word and all that hinges on our acceptance of it, feeding from it and rebuking Satan with it, if Satan could change the Word, a word at a time, a translation at a time, a generation at a time, eventually it would lose all its power over him and become empty and of no effect.

Can you see what I am trying to say here? There are certain elements of God's Word that hold the power and, apart from these elements of power, the Word of God becomes just another book, empty of changing power, empty of the rebuking power over Satan. Satan could go and come with a free run of our lives, our homes and our churches. God has given us power. God has given us His Son. But man gets confused so easily. The Cain and Abel story is a good example of just how easily we can become confused.

The Word of God must continue to hold the vital elements of power to pull down the strongholds in our lives. "Casting down imaginations, and every high thing that exalteth itself against the knowledge of God, and bringing into captivity every thought to the obedience of Christ." II Corinthians 10:5.

You see, God has instilled these power elements in the Word, just as the blood in your body has elements of power and disease-fighting ability. If you allow this blood to be stripped of its elements of power, it simply becomes just another liquid. *This is Satan's old deception, not to completely get rid of God's Word, but to simply change the power of it.*

Let me demonstrate to you how Satan is using the same trick on our generation that he used on Eve, and tried to use on Jesus. I am only going to give you a few examples in a few categories, but there are literally hundreds that could be given. I only hope to give you the idea and you can then research the rest for yourself.

As a good starter, worship – whom are we to worship?

Subject: Philippians 3:3

KJV   *"Worship God"*
NIV, NASB   *"Worship."*

This is a good example to start with. It seems very harmless. But remember Mark 4:15, when Jesus said, "Where the word is sown; but when they have heard, Satan cometh immediately and taketh away the word." Satan is simply removing one block at a time. Please be alert and look for the enemy's fingerprints. You just may find his prints on the new minority manuscript Bibles.

Another very interesting subject is Satan himself. It is very interesting how, through the new translators, he has tried to completely change his image.

Subject: Satan-Lucifer (Isaiah 14:12-7)

"How art thou fallen from heaven, O Lucifer, son of the morning! How art thou cut down to the ground, which didst weaken the nations! For thou hast said in thine heart, I will ascend into heaven, I will exalt my throne above the stars of God: I will sit also upon the mount of the congregation, in the sides of the north: I will ascend above the heights of the clouds; I will be like the most High.

Yet thou shalt be brought down to hell, to the sides of the put. They that see thee shall narrowly look upon thee, and consider thee saying, Is this the man that made the earth to tremble, that did shake kingdoms; That made the world a wilderness, and destroyed the cities thereof; That opened not the house of his prisoners?"

In Lucifer's boastful words, "I will be like the most High," the new person he wished to pursue included the response of worship from whosoever would. This is seen in his appeal to Jesus recorded in Luke 4:7. Unfortunately, his ambition will be fulfilled as seen in Rev. 13:4 "and they worshiped the dragon."

The public relations campaign required to transform the public's image of Satan, from his true evil character to one which would inspire worship, is monumental.   It pivots upon the transformation of his identity.

Historically, Isaiah 14 has been used as the singular biography of Lucifer, shedding unique light upon the "mystery of iniquity."   In verse twelve, Lucifer is in heaven; in verse fifteen, Satan is in hell. The intervening verses expose his pride in the five "I wills," each a rung on the ladder in his descent into hell.

These passages must be the object of Satan's desires and, consequently, his opposition. They reveal his arrogance, his responsibility for much of the world's misery, and his end. He is indicted as sounded in Ezekiel, 28, but is unnamed and designated "the anointed cherub."

His ambition is to be "like the most High," and these verses sweep away that illusion, presenting him as transparent.   To hold that he would not grapple with the word "Lucifer" until it was securely removed from such an unflattering context and replanted into a "like the most High" context is naiveté.

Fait accompli, the feat is accomplished in all new Bible versions; the KJV remains uncorrupted.

NIV How you have fallen from heaven, O morning star, son of the dawn...but you are brought down to the grave.

NAS How you have fallen from heaven, O star of the morning, son of the dawn...you will be thrust down to Sheol.

KJV How art thou fallen from heaven, O Lucifer, son of the morning!...Yet thou shalt be brought down to hell.

Twentieth century versions have removed the name Lucifer, thereby eliminating the only reference to him in the entire Bible. The word Lucifer then falls to a realm of the poets and writers of mythology and ceases to be an identifiable character of biblical origin. He is thereby divorced from the truth concerning himself. In John 8:44 Jesus said, "for he (the devil) is a liar, and the father of it." He can now have whatever characteristic he desires.

The change in new versions does not spring from the original Hebrew language, but the theology of the new version editors. The NIV wording parallels exactly the view expressed by NIV committee member R. Laird Harris. He asserts that Isaiah 14 is not about Lucifer and his descent to hell, but about a king from Babylon and his interment in the grave.

An examination of the original Hebrew will dispel any illusion that "morning star" is an acceptable substitute for the word Lucifer. The Hebrew is "helel, helel, ben schacher," which is accurately translated "Lucifer, son of the morning." The NIV and NASB give an English translation as if the Hebrew said, "shachar, kokal, ben shachar" or "morning star, son of the morning dawn." Yet the word for star (kokab) appears nowhere in the text. Also, morning appears *only once* as the KJV shows, not twice as new versions indicate. The word "kokab" is translated as "star" dozens of times by NIV translators, "morning" or "dawn" is likewise used hundreds of times. New version editors know "boger kokab" as "morning star," since it is used in Job 38:7. If God had intended to communicate "morning star," he would have repeated it here. *The word He chose, "helel" appears nowhere else in the Old Testament, just as "Lucifer" appears nowhere else.*

Let's look at other examples of problems in the new versions. As they are listed, think of the difference made by the change when compared. I am not going to elaborate much on them, but simply list them.

In John 4:23 the NASB substitutes "bow" (a position of the body) for "worship (an attitude of the spirit) in the following verses.

NASB		KJV
bowed down	Matt. 9:16	worshiped him
bowed down	Matt. 8:2	worshiped him
bowed down	Matt. 15:25	worshiped him
bowed down	Matt. 20:20	worshipping him
falling down prostrate	Matt. 18:26	worshiped him
bowed down	Mark 5:6	worshiped him

The Name of Christ Jesus shortened

NIV, NASB, etc.		KJV
This is not the Christ, is it?	John 4:29	Is not this the Christ?
Jesus	Acts 19:4	Christ Jesus
Jesus	I Cor. 9:1	Jesus Christ
Jesus	1 John 1:7	Jesus Christ
Omitted	John 6:69	Thou art that Christ
Lord Jesus	Eph. 1:15	Lord Jesus Christ
Omitted	Romans 1:3	Jesus Christ our Lord
the gospel	Romans 1:6	the gospel of Christ
I can do everything through him	Phil. 4:13	I can do all things through Christ
Let this Christ	Mark 15:32	Let Christ

See the subtle changes in references to Christ Jesus, our only Lord and Christ? These references do not seem like much, but read on, please.

What about Jesus? Is He God?

NIV, NASB, etc. translated Phil 2:6 "(Jesus) did not consider equality with God something to be grasped." But the KJV translated this verse "(Jesus) thought it not robbery to be equal with God."

Quite a difference! From KJV, where Jesus thought it not robbery for Him to be equal with God, to NIV and NASB, where Jesus couldn't be equal with God. Can you not see the extreme demotion of the person of Jesus to someone less than God Himself?

The defenders of this change say, "But it is that way in the Greek." The truth is that it is not that way in the Majority, the Textus Receptus. These types of problems were probably the reason the minority manuscripts were rejected for 1,600 years, coupled with the missing sections from Revelation 1 which declares Jesus to be the Alpha and Omega. It is very evident that the minority manuscripts have a problem with declaring Jesus and God one and the same. They totally omit this statement by John.

The New Contemporary Version leaves out the proclamation of who is talking almost totally. Does this not bother you? It sure bothers me!

Jude 1:4

NIV, NASB   *"the only Master and Lord Jesus Christ"*

KJV   *"the only Lord God, and our Lord Jesus Christ"*

Jesus here has been demoted from God to Master. This is quite a change, don't you think?

NIV, NASB, etc.		KJV
Let this Christ	Mark 15:32	Let Christ

Is he *a* Son or **The** Son (Rev. 14:14)

NIV, NASB, etc.   *"sitting on a cloud was one like a son of man"*

KJV   *"upon the cloud one sat like unto the Son of man"*

Many other references do the same thing to the Son of God. I will list a few: Rev. 1:1, John 6:19, Matt. 27:54, Mark 15:39, Dan. 3:25, Mark 1:1, Mark 12:16, Matt 8:25, etc. But one that really stands out is Acts 17:31. The NIV and NASB translated it, "He will judge the world in righteousness through a man." But the KJV translated the same verse, "he will judge the world in righteousness by that man."

Is the world to be judged by *a* man or *that specific* man? In summary of the name game, let's look and compare!

KJV	New Versions
Lucifer	morning star
Jehovah	Lord
Holy One of Israel	Spirit
Holy Ghost	Spirit
Lord Jesus Christ	Lord

Some would say, "This isn't important; we know who will judge the world, or who is who in the Bible." All right, who said in the 50's in America that removing creation and replacing it with evolution wouldn't affect our children? "We know who our creator is." I say, "You do and I do, but will my grandchildren know if they are missing the solid, unchangeable truth?"

What about the message of the Gospel?

I will list many verses where the NIV and NASB changed the message of the gospel from **The** Gospel Message to **A** Gospel Message: John 6:68, Rev. 14:6, 2 John 1:1, Acts 14:27, Titus 11:4, etc.

From **the** God to **a** God; Daniel 3:25, Acts 14:15, 1 Thes. 1:9, James 2:19.

Are we saved by works or by grace?

Luke 21:19 NIV says, "By standing firm you will gain life" (save yourself). The KVJ says, "In your patience possess ye your souls."

1 Peter 2:2 NASB says, "Ye may grow in respect to salvation." But the KJV says, "ye may grow thereby" (as a result of).

See also John 5:22, Acts 18:5, Gal. 5:20, 1 Tim. 4:12, John 3:36, Romans 11:32, Heb. 3:18, Heb. 4:6, Heb. 4:11, Rom 15:31, etc.

Are we commanded or instructed?

NIV,NASB,etc.		KJV
instruct	Matt. 10:5	commanded
precepts	Mark 7:7	commandments
God said	Matt. 15:4	God commanded
respect	Matt. 21:37	reverence
instructed	Mark 6:7	commanded
instructed	1 Tim. 4:11	commanded
reverence	1 Pet. 3:15	fear

Etcetera, etcetera, etcetera...

Blasphemy

The word "blasphemy" has been weakened to say something *less than* blasphemy. Col. 3:8, Mark 7:22, Matt. 15:19, Matt. 7:22, Titus 2:7, etc.

Fornication

The word "fornication" (very specifically a sin of sexuality) is replaced by the word "immorality" (could mean anything, depending on the person and his or her view of what is moral). Again, the specifics are taken away.

NIV, NASB, etc.		KJV
Omitted	Romans 1:29	fornication
immorality	1 Cor. 5:1	fornication
immorality	1 Cor. 6:13	fornication
immorality	2 Cor. 12:21	fornication
immorality	Ephesians 5:1	fornication
immorality	Colossians 3:5	fornication
immorality	Rev. 2:14	fornication
immorality	Rev. 2:20	fornication
act immoral	1 Cor. 10:8	commit fornication
immorality	Galatians 5:19	adultery and fornication

There are many more. Fornication is a sexual sin. Immorality may or may not be. Immorality is a word used in general terms depending on what is considered immoral to a culture and society. Morals change drastically with culture. Can you see the big problems coming as a result of this and other watered-down words?

What about omitted verses?

Examine Acts 8:35 in the NIV and NASB. They have totally omitted the latter part of the verse. What does this verse say? "I believe that Jesus Christ is the Son of God." Yes, totally omitted. This is a big missing section in Acts. The statement omitted is the part that declares why the man is ready to be baptized. Totally missing!

This is a real problem. The NIV is 64,098 words shorter than the KJV, simply because of deleted verses, phrases and words. A few are listed here: Matt. 5:44; Mark 11:25, Romans 13:9, Rev. 1:11, 8, 18, Mark 9:44, Mark 9:46, Mark 6:11.

There is so much more than could be said about the word changes, deletions and weakened phrases. The phrases and verses so often have been weakened. Just one major example is the world "fornication" being changed to "immorality." The specifics are gone. More and more you will notice, if you really want to know.

The Fruit of a Weakened Word

I don't think you or I need to look far to find the fruit of a weakened Bible. A weaker manuscript makes a weaker Bible. Weaker Bibles bring forth weaker Christians. Weaker Christians make for weaker churches. Weaker churches bring forth weaker convictions. Weaker convictions bring weaker morality, in the pulpit, pews, homes and society. If the church cannot stand strong on absolute truth, how can we expect society to do so? Therefore, it's a simple case of cause and effect. The Bible is the power source for absolute truth, morality, etc. Without it, we are going down. Simply put, no unchanging truth, no future.

Today in the churches across America, you must search high and low to find a preacher or congregation that really believes the Bible to be the final authority. The simple truth is that, under the arms of the liberal, moderate Bible preacher, or so-called Christian is a minority manuscript Bible nearly every time. I challenge you to look and see.

When Darwin pitched his theory onto the education scene, he was simply laughed at and written off. No one would have thought that his conjured-up thoughts on the subject of man's origin would have amounted to much. But look at the situation now. Now we see without question the devastation caused by the acceptance of evolution into our education systems.

When O'Hair went before the judge to remove prayer from the halls of the public school, no one thought she could do so. Also, I might add, when she did, no one thought it would matter, seeing most families respected God and would teach the values and godly teaching at home. But look at the school zone today, absent God's presence.

We are now experiencing the beginning rumbles of a devastating tidal wave as a result of the new translation dilemma. On a personal note, I was testifying before a committee in Maryland two years ago to try to stop the State of Maryland from treating homosexuality as a race, handicap, etc. They were trying to give special status to the homosexual people because of their sexual preference. Therefore, I went with others to try to hold back that decision. I was preceded in testimony by many Bible-carrying Christians who continued to tell the committee there was nothing in their Bible that said that homosexuality was bad. Of course, they were reading and carrying one of the new translations that had been reworded, and words like "sodomy" had been either removed or reworded.

The Southern Baptist Convention has been fighting for the inerrancy of Scripture for the last 25 years. But the ones who are fighting to water down the Word and push forth liberalism are always the new translation carriers. This is just the way it is. I did not make it so; I simply am telling you what I and you can observe.

Simply put, bad fruit is surfacing. But what about the future? If we are having a hard time now as a result of weaker Bibles, and this only for 100 years, and with a few translations and changes, what do you think will be the Christian values and truth in 40 more years? The old conservatives are dying away. The tidal wave is coming – do you hear its rumbling?

The Need for Absolute Authority

The need for absolute authority is so needed in any society. We do not need to look far to find the devastation befallen our American society with a people who cannot find truth. In the new, modern American classroom, truth is irrelevant. The sad thing is that the leaders do not even see the need for absolute truth. This same dilemma was present in the Roman society. This was evidenced in the conversation between Jesus and Pilate as Pilate asked Jesus that golden question, "What is Truth?"

In John 18:36, Jesus is being questioned just before He is crucified. Let me let you read this small conversation for yourself:

> *Verses 36-38 "Jesus answered, My kingdom is not of this world: if my kingdom were of this world, then would my servants fight, that I should not be delivered to the Jews: but now is my kingdom not from hence. 37 Pilate therefore said unto him, Art thou a king then? Jesus answered, Thou sayest that I am a king. To this end was I born, and for this cause came I into the world, that I should bear witness unto the truth. Every one that is of the truth heareth my voice. 38 Pilate saith unto him, What is truth?"*

This was and is a vital question. What is truth? A question even more important for today is the question, "Does truth exist at all?" Jesus said it did and He came to bear witness of it. If truth exists then what is it? Where is it? Where is that ultimate, unchanging foundation that is ultimate truth that is always the same and never moves? The only unchanging truth is the Word of God. But in our day the rewriting of the Scriptures has now even brought *that* into question when we read the Word of God and it states the verse in a different, weaker way. My question is to you: where is truth going? We know truth exists. We know that truth is relevant. But how far from truth will we allow those translators to take the ultimate truth of God's word before we say something? Maybe the guards of the Word of God, (the Christian leaders) do not feel as though truth is important. I say to all who read this that truth is relevant—absolute truth.

In the King James translations, when the translators needed to add a word to make the sentence sound more acceptable in English, they would *italicize* the word to let you know that they had added something, but that is not true in our modern translations. I believe it is because they feel the *idea* is inspired, not the *word-for-word* translation. Remember the conservative and liberal battle over truth? The liberal says that the *idea* Jesus gave us is inspired, not the *word-for-word Scriptures.* But the conservatives stood on, and fought for, the word-for-word inerrancy of Scriptures. Remember that? What happened to those conservatives who, in the 80s and 90s, stood and proclaimed the inerrancy of scripture, word-for-word? Where are they now?

I contend that the secondary manuscript translations have lulled them to sleep and quietly convinced them that the word-for-word translation is not important. But my question is: what will be the next stage in this absolute truth dilemma? What will be the next generation of Christian leaders' response? Will they be weaker still? Will this beginning weakness continue to snowball? What will be the effect of the new Christian leaders who are not informed of the manuscript switch? Will this apathy toward the word-for-word translation continue to manifest itself in an ever-increasing willingness to allow word changes, paraphrases, word deletions? I ask you not, "Where is truth?" I ask you, "Where are you and I going to allow truth to go? Where is truth going?"

Now we hear statements when discussing a doctrinal truth like, "It depends on the translation you read," or, "Which Bible is *the* Bible, anyway?" or "My Bible doesn't say *that*," or "My Bible doesn't say it *that way*."

I could give you many personal illustrations of how this is already affecting society and the church. While I was discussing the Church with a State of Maryland representative, she asked, "Which Bible is *the* Bible, anyway? Your group has many Bibles that disagree." I also remember the state meeting before those considering "special rights" for homosexuals. I was in a Senate meeting discussing another problem with the state over making laws respecting homosexuality, and other preachers there with liberal translations stood and said, "My Bible doesn't say what his says." See what I mean?

Without absolute truth we are doomed. The world has lost truth. Therefore, science, history, psychology, etc. have no solid foundations. Even in colleges today we find people who can't even say Hitler was wrong. This is a result of no absolute truth. But at least we have had a church empowered with truth. But now we are going to lose absolute truth in the churches without action from God's leaders. You may not believe this, but just wait and see. If the warnings by myself and others are not heeded, what can the world do without absolute truth on that planet. This is what I call the tidal wave to come!

The Good Men Dilemma

Let me say what I am *not* saying. I am not saying that everyone who reads or preaches from a translation other than the KJV is a liberal. I am saying that the next generation is more likely to be so. Also, I am saying that those who use the new translations are not informed nor do they see the problems ahead or they would be supporting me in my burden to call attention to this dilemma. Some are people who have heard and refuse to face the facts, but most I say are simply not informed. But these good people with good intentions do not change the results of cause and effect. They do not change the fruit growing as a result of weaker, paraphrased Bibles. I have written letters to some of our key leaders in these churches. They simply tell me that they are not informed in this area of study, and that they do not have the time to become informed. But this is like saying they are too busy to check the oil in their car because they are too busy driving it. If they do not take the time to check the oil you know it's only a matter of time until trouble will be upon them, and then it's too late to check it; the damage will already be done.

Some of these leaders tell me that they agree with me, but do not know what to do about it. Some say they see what I am saying, but do not think it will affect society or the church that badly.

On and on the responses come from good men with good intentions, but who are asleep at the wheel, so to speak. Jesus said, "No man can enter into a strong man's house, and spoil his goods, except he will first bind the strong man; and then he will spoil his house," Mark 3:27. How can we not see the application of this verse here in this tidal wave dilemma we have been discussing?

There are many good men who have been bound by their Bible professors, tradition, personal preference, liberal Seminaries, lack of knowledge or just simply being too busy. Whatever the reason, good men or bad men, the results will still be the same if we do not come forth and take our rightful place on God's wall and *defend the truth and purity of God's Word.* From the Garden of Eden to the temptations of Christ, Satan has always changed a word here and there to distort truth and confuse God's people. His tricks are the same. I just cannot believe more people cannot see this happening.

The man who is sitting in his house tied up with whatever, while his family is being destroyed, is no different than us if we do not get out of our comfort zones, find the truth, and do it—whatever it costs. I cannot seem to find men with enough courage or willingness to even raise an eyebrow. If they do, they simply look at me as a troublemaker, when I really am just trying to fight for the purity of God's Word and hold back this devastating tidal wave to come.

Conclusion

I hope you can understand why I am so disturbed about this dilemma of new translations. I can see the same thing happening to the biblical foundation that happened to the science and history foundations in America. This foundation we cannot afford to lose. We couldn't afford to lose the other two. But this will be an unrecoverable mistake, a tidal wave.

This tidal wave to come began to mount from 1881 and is still mounting power. 1881 was the Revised Standard Version translated from new manuscripts. These manuscripts were a product of Hort and Westcott. Hort and Westcott were two men whom most church wouldn't even allow to preach in their pulpits, from what information I can gather about them.

These modern translations were affected greatly by modern science, art, and modern thinking, and Charles Darwin's day. Yes, Charles Darwin was there. I want you to understand the influence Darwin and his type had on these new versions.

Critics of those like myself continue to say that we KJV lovers are just narrow-minded people who refuse to understand, that before the 1611 KJV, there were other English versions. But my answer to them is that the other English versions were not translated from these Westcott and Hort promoted manuscripts. Also, these new translations seem to be designed to sell but the earlier versions were made to save. I'm not saying they will not help people find Christ. But I am saying that they were created by people and priced to sell, copyrighted to sell, etc. A good example of this was the 1996 attempt by the NIV publishers to produce a no=gender Bible. The only reason they didn't was because they felt the public was, as they said, not ready for it.

Hort, Westcott, Darwin's influence, money, copyrights, interdenominational translators, cause and effect, minority manuscripts, liberal promoters. What am I trying to say? Weak Work, weak future, and a destructive today wave to come.

We have a Holy Bible. We have a Bible given to us by God's hand, preserved by God's hand, blood bought.

The OT Jews felt so strongly about God's Word, they carefully and humbly wrote the name of God with fear and trembling. They scribed every letter carefully and counted each letter on a page to see if they could have miscopied one letter. If so, they would throw the work away. They labored hard and long, and with holy hands.

The Accuracy of the Bible Manuscripts

Over the last four thousand years, Jewish scribes, and later Christian scribes, were very careful to correctly copy and transmit the original manuscripts and sacred Scriptures without any significant error. The Jewish scribes who carefully copies out by hand the manuscripts of the Old Testament were called "Masoretic" from the Hebrew word "wall" or "fence." Their extreme care in meticulously counting the letters of the Bible created a "fence around the Law" to defend its absolute accuracy. These pages were so precise in counting the exact number of letters in the scriptures, that they were able to pinpoint the middle verse of Genesis which is, "And by the sword shalt thou live, and shalt serve thy brother; and it shall come to pass when thou shalt have the dominion, that thou shalt break his yoke from off thy neck" (Genesis 27:40). When a scribe completed his copy, a master examiner would painstakingly count every individual letter to confirm that there were no errors in the newly-copied manuscript. If an error was found, the mistaken copy was destroyed to prevent it from ever being used as a master copy in the future.

As a proof of the incredible accuracy of this transmission through the centuries, consider the Masoretic and Yemenite translations of the Torah. Over a millennium ago, Yemenite Jews were separated from their Jewish brethren in the Middle East and Europe. Despite separate transmissions and copying of their Torah manuscripts, a thousand years later, only nine Hebrew letters out of 304,805 letters in the Yemenite Torah manuscript, differ from the accepted Hebrew Masoretic text of the Torah. Not one of these nine variant letters in the Yemenite Torah change the meaning of a significant word. This astonishing fact proves how exceptionally careful, over a thousand-year period, Jewish scribes were copying their original Torah manuscripts. God has carefully preserved the original text of His sacred Scriptures throughout the last three thousand years, enabling us to have confidence that we still possess the inspired Word of God. The prophet Isaiah declared that the Word of God is eternal, "The grass withereth, the flower fadeth: but the word of our God shall stand forever"

(Isaiah 40:8). In the New Testament, Jesus Himself confirmed the indestructibility of His Holy Word. "For verily I say unto you, Till heaven and earth pass, one jot or one tittle shall in no wise pass from the law, till all be fulfilled" (Matthew 5:18).

Dr. Samuel Johnson's suggestion, "Keep your friendships in repair," was excellent advice regarding our relationship to our Bible as well as for our human relationships. Our relationship with the Word of God needs to be cared for just as much as our friendships. We need to respect God's Holy Word and handle it with care and love. We can enjoy the unchanging companionship of God expressed through His divine Word even when we are separated from human friends by distance or death. Our Bibles that show signs of wear and tear reveal our love and use of them. While our experiences, or possessions, and our relationships constantly undergo change throughout the years we can return again and again to the unchanging Word of God as a solid foundation for our faith that will never change.[lvii]

The care and protecting of the Word have always been a priority, many even giving their lives to keep it sacred and pure. Their care and sacrifice is what brought us this pure and powerful Word of God. How can we allow our generation to treat the Word of God with such carelessness? How can translators change words, phrases, leave out words, verses, parts of verses, paraphrase statements and etc., and we say *nothing?* I cannot believe our 1990s men of God have so been influenced to keep quiet about this today wave mounting. I cannot understand why we Bible-believers who know the power of the Scriptures say nothing when Scripture is being treated so carelessly. It must be that our men of God are poorly informed or misinformed. This has been my experience. When I have tried to share my concerns about this problem, I cannot find people or even preachers informed enough on this subject to even discuss it. I am writing this book to try to inform and stir God's men to search and see if I am not saying truth. If we do not stop and search out this dilemma, by the time we see there is a problem it's going to be too late to fix it; just like the science, evolution dilemma, and the Christian heritage dilemma, as well. When the damage was being done, no one would listen. Now we can see the devastation left by those errors. But now is the time to see this tidal wave coming and stop it. Rise up, men of God! Take time to look at God's Word through the eyes of a guard and help proclaim the need to stop Satan from rewriting God's Word.

The evidence we have seen of the flawed Hort-Westcott, Minority manuscripts, shows us such disagreement—even to the point it has been said, that if it were translated word-for-word in its original for all would reject the product that resulted! Word changing, weakening Bibles—it is getting worse every year. The evidence is plain to see and overwhelming. I feel like a man who has found a hundred-dollar bill lying on the ground in the middle of a crowded street, looking up and wondering why someone hasn't already seen it and picked it up.

The problem is so plain simple. I keep talking, reading and asking questions, thinking that someone will tell me the hidden reason why this has been overlooked this long. But after years of trying, I can only say the world just doesn't know. The ones who promote and use them just do not know. But now, you know!

If the foundation by destroyed, what can the righteous do?
--Psalm 11:3

_____
_____
_____
_____

CHAPTER FOUR

THE CHANGING TIDE
GETTING READY FOR A THIRD GREAT AWAKENING

"If my people, which are called by my name,
shall humble themselves, and pray, and seek my face,
and turn from their wicked ways; then will I hear from
heaven, and will forgive their sin,
and will heal their land."
-- II CHRONICLES 7:14

I. THE FREQUENCY OF GREAT AWAKENINGS

The previous sections of this book painted a pretty bleak picture. If things continue as they are going, America is no doubt sinking. The loss of creation and Christian Heritage has dealt a staggering blow to our society. The fruits of this loss are everywhere. The most devastating of all is the tidal wave of watered-down Bibles. This seems to be the stone that will seal our grave.

Let's think for just a moment. God has always reserved Himself a remnant. When Elijah cried out to God from a cave, saying he was the only servant of God left, God reminded him that He had always reserved a remnant. He had 4,000 who had not yet bowed to Baal.

The First Great Awakening

Before the first Great Awakening in the early 1700s, the colonies were in great need of revival. The future of America was about to be shaped. God needed leaders to establish America for His purpose in the generations ahead. He needed men and women with integrity and conviction but, most of all, a deep respect for the Word of God and the God of the Word.

Therefore, God burdened a remnant of preachers. These men, John and Charles Wesley, George Whitefield, Jonathan Edwards and others with sacrifice and passion preached in the Great Awakening I. These godly men preached all up and down the Eastern seaboard preparing the people for the revolution, and preparing the leaders for a constitution that would keep America in check for years to come. This great awakening is what made men like George Washington, Thomas Jefferson, Noah Webster and many others the great founders of American freedom. One cannot study American History and not see the influence of this great revival on our founders. When the need for a remnant was there, God raised up a remnant.

The Second Great Awakening

Again, at the turn of the 1900s, America needed to move forward in its call to God's purpose. Hindered by the sins of the day, worldliness and simple selfishness, America needed revival. America was going through a time of growth and greed. As big industry was taking root, farmers began to leave their roots, taking higher-paying jobs away from their families and their homes.

America was on the verge of a great explosion of growth and prosperity. That's when sin seems to thrive the most. Therefore, that's when revival is needed the most. God called forth a group of men and women with convictions and a love for God and His Word. The remnant was called, and they answered. D.L. Moody, Charles Spurgeon, Billy Sunday, and many others were the preachers who, with power, established the basis for America in the 1900s. This is called the Great Awakening II.

Will History Repeat Itself?

It is now 100 years later. We are now past 2020. Again, our great nation needs a move of God. Again, we need a new step in our calling if we are to survive. The question is, will there be a Great Awakening III? The question to you is, is there a remnant left, and are you a part of the ones who have not bowed down before Baal?

Now, I want to remind you that, when God burdened Whitefield, he didn't realize all that was going to happen because of his life. When the Lord burdened Moody, uneducated as he was, butchering the English language everywhere he went (just as I am prone to do), he was so empowered of God that people could not deny that the power of God was upon him. He didn't realize that he was going to do with his life. And I want to tell you something: none of these people—not even Moses himself—could fathom what God was going to do with their commitment.

Today it's the same way. What will God do with just one man or one woman's commitment? God is calling leadership today! All over this nation and the world there are little revival fires beginning, spurts here and spurts there, and when He calls one, He calls others. I know that God is about to do something.

Recently, in Columbia, a terrible earthquake rocked that whole country. This is just one of many examples that God can do what He wants to. In America, I don't know whether it's going to be a financial earthquake, I don't know whether it's going to be a financial earthquake, I don't know whether it's going to be disease, I don't know what it's going to take to turn people's attention back to Him. But we, as God's people, have all the tools to work with and we've got to use them! But, unless we use them with our whole heart, we're going to have to have something to break us.

I think the Civil War is really what broke us to get us ready for the Second Great Awakening. It humbled America. As a result, Great Awakening II came on. I don't know what it's going to take for Great Awakening III, but I know we're a part of it! And I don't know what's going to happen tomorrow, but we've got to prepare for today.

A Crisis in Leadership

The problem is that in most churches in America, 20% of the members do all the work—all the giving, all the teaching, all the involvement. We have some areas that need prayer—we have some things that need to be done! If we're going to do what God has asked us to do, it's going to take all our commitment, not just 20%.

The struggle we have today in our Christian society is gathering leadership. The trouble we have with young people today in school is developing leaders, not followers, and not only in our young people, but in our homes. So often in today's time we say, "God, You're a great Santa Claus. You make my life happy. You make my life what it ought to be. You make me comfortable." The Lord has, indeed, done everything for us! He has given us everything we have, everything we are. We need to come to the place where we say, "Lord, what can I do for *You*?" Personal surrender is what must take place in our lives for us to truly have the victory we need—for us to be able to see God's hand in our ministry, and to impact lives for Christ.

If we're serving God, it's His mission. It's His promises and presence that really counts; it's His appointment that really matters. The driving motivation should be an appointment with God. When we look Him in the fact what are we going to say? Are we going to be able to look at the Lord and know we were faithful with all He gave us and all He asked of us, or are we going to stand there in shame with tall the provisions He gave us to use for His kingdom and say, "I'm sorry, but I wasted them?"

If you're going to be a proper leader for God, you need people. You need instruction from the Spirit of God, and from other teachers. Moses told the Lord, "Lord, I just cannot do this job. I am just not big enough!" One of the number one things that needs to be a part of your character for you to be able to do a good job for God is to acknowledge your weakness, for when we are weak, He is strong. When sin doth abound, so grace doth more abound. People who serve God must realize that *they can't*, but **God can**! God has a calling just for you! Moses had his and Abraham had his, Wesley and Whitefield had theirs and we have ours. We're past 2020 now, and we need Great Awakening III. But it is going to take from our hearts a commitment and a focus beyond what we now have.

In Exodus chapter four, we see that Moses had a crisis of belief. He was self-conscious (a form of pride—fear of not measuring up, of being rejected based on his own abilities). After God demonstrated the miraculous signs that he would work through Moses to validate Moses' authority and to authenticate his calling, Moses still balked at God's calling:

> *And Moses said unto the Lord, O my Lord, I am not eloquent, neither heretofore, nor since thou hast spoken unto thy servant: but I am*

slow of speech, and of a slow tongue. And the Lord said unto him, Who hath made man's mouth? or who maketh the dumb, or deaf, or the seeing, or the blind? have not I the Lord? Now therefore go, and I will be with thy mouth, and teach thee what thou shalt say. And he said, O my Lord, send, I pray thee, by the hand of him whom thou wilt send. And the anger of the Lord was kindled against Moses, and he said, Is not Aaron the Levite thy brother? I know that he can speak well. And also, behold, he cometh forth to meet thee: and when he seeth thee, he will be glad in his heart. And thou shalt speak unto him, and put words in his mouth: and I will be with thy mouth, and with his mouth, and will teach you what ye shall do. And he shall be thy spokesman unto the people: and he shall be, even he shall be to thee instead of a mouth, and thou shalt be to him instead of God. And thou shalt take this rod in thine hand, wherewith thou shalt do signs (Exodus 4:10-17).

God will always give you what you need. For Moses it was Aaron, and God has an Aaron for you. If you don't have one, seek God and find one. Find someone who will spiritually work with you, someone who will spiritually pray with you, somebody that will walk with you day by day. You need one. Men, find a godly man. Women, find a goodly woman. Get a mentor, a prayer partner, somebody to share your burdens with. God will give you your Aaron.

When Moses finally said yes, he began the calling that God had given him that no one could fathom doing; it was a total impossibility. And we may feel that way when we look at our world. You say, "Pastor, this place has gone to pot!" We're in such a bad shape that our leadership in Washington, D.C., is a soap opera! There's no humility down there at all. There *are* a few down there that are on their knees—because God, in His providential mercy, always reserves a remnant.

Overall, we are in trouble in America. We have walked into a world of distress and destruction. With the 2019-2020 days of Covid-19, racial riots in the streets, and liberal government officials, one might think that America would have already come to themselves and cried out for revival, but we may have gone too far. Great revivals are born out of the Word of God, and it just may be that Satan has delivered a devastating blow to America. Satan has always been good at altering the words of God and twisting confidence in God as the authority. In Genesis 2-3, Adam and Eve were beguiled by the serpent by his changing just a word or two. He again tried to confuse Jesus as he tempted Him in the wilderness of Judea (recorded in Luke changer 4). We in America are now suffering from our enemy's handiwork as he has altered just a few choice areas in the many new Bible translations that our Bible leaders are now reading. This has a challenging effect, as many of the responsible men of God are not confident in the Bible they hold in their hands. The Great Awakening III is needed, but we are truly at God's mercy. The good news is that God has always saved a remnant. He has always had Himself a group of servants that has not surrendered to the enemy. He has been known to use donkeys to deliver His truth. Therefore, I am proud to just be one of His "donkeys."

But with God it will all work together for good. Now, I don't want to die; I don't want you to die; I don't want to be sick and I don't want my children hungry...I don't want these things to happen, but I want what God wants. And if it will take that to bring America back to where it ought to be, to bring us to kneeling before God like we ought to, then so be it. When we, as a nation, get in trouble, the pro-abortion mouths and homosexual activists won't have an audience because people won't have time for it. The advocates for sin are silenced because no one has time for those people when survival is foremost in their minds. They, too, are just sinners that need to be saved. When tragedy comes and people get humbled, they don't have time for all that "I've got rights" stuff, it just won't work anymore— when people are in trouble.

Covid-19 has shut the world down. It is not just one country over another one, but the world. It is just an example as to how far people will go to be safe. The sad thing is that, after all we have been through, we are still not in revival. But God is still able to bring people to their knees if He so desires.

However, Peter tells us in 2 Peter 3 that "in the last days there will be scoffers walking after their own lusts..." Paul told Timothy in 2 Timothy 3, "This know also, that in the last days perilous times will come. For men shall be lovers of their own selves ..."

We are praying for a Great Awakening, but it just may be that we have moved into the phase of the end of the Church age. We are praying for an Awakening for the Church to be able to take advantage of the open world to the Gospel through the internet as well as other means, but we just do not know. One thing is sure, though; when the Word of God has lost its power to change hearts, that is when God steps out and makes a move. Remember that Noah Preached over 100 years without one convert outside his family, and Lot was called a preacher of righteousness by Peter. 2 Peter 2:7 says, "...just Lot, vexed with the filthy conversation of the wicked" when he was in Sodom. God had to destroy Sodom because no one would heed his words. It just tells us that, when the word of God being preached falls on deaf ears, the end is near, even at the door!

II.   THE FOUNDATIONS OF REVIVAL

I can see that there were three major characteristics that brought on the first two Great Awakenings. Even the reformation was built on these three cornerstones. History boldly declares these three foundations of yesterday. It is seemingly safe to say the third awakening will not happen without them.   If the third Great

Awakening is to come the remnant will be burdened in these three areas.

Power # 1 The Word of God Unquestioned:

The previous revivals or awakenings could not have happened without absolute faith in the Word of God and the God of the Word. We could not then, nor can we now, expect to have a genuine awakening without a solid foundation.

Let me share just a word of explanation here. Many are seeking to stir the people of God. People are praying for revival, talking about revival, encouraging revival. But any stirring that is based on anything other than the authority and foundation of Scripture will shortly dwindle away.

The responsibility of revival is squarely on the shoulders of God's men. But God's men are wasting their time and energy if they are trying to establish a move of God without the Word of God. God's Word is the pillar for power. Revival is a product of Bible power. True revival is deep. It calls people to serve God with sacrificial love. True revival only comes through true repentance. True revival calls people to love the Word and the God of the Word. True revival is a fruit of people who preach the unchanging Word of God without any variance or error.

The revival of Josiah in II Kings 12 and Nehemiah in Nehemiah 8, the first and second American Awakenings and even the Protestant reformations all were a product of love and respect for the Word of God and the God of the Word. The words, "Thus saith the Lord," brought humility and broken hearts. Therefore, history proclaims the necessity of God's Word and its unmovable and uncompromising truth. I hope you will see the necessity of this book and your actions after you have read it.

My prayer is that you can understand, after becoming aware of these truths, that we are not just talking about a revival in the country or in the world; we are talking about a revival of the heart as well. We are talking about a personal revival! How can this be? How does one become personally revived? The Bible tells us how personal revival comes. History tells us how personal revival comes. When we are given a true diet of the truth, God begins to do something in our hearts. It was like that when Martin Luther and William Tyndale were reading the Word of God, became convicted, and settled the fact of their own personal faith. Then they became burdened to do whatever it took to do God's will and come forth in their specific lives to proclaim truth. Let me remind you that Martin Luther was trying to become a follower of Christ by knowing about God and doing things for God and realized, when he read the manuscripts of the Bible, that Salvation comes to humans by faith in the finished work of Jesus Christ on the cross and the wonderful display of God's power by His personal resurrection. Martin Luther declared that he was made right by trusting on the finished work of Jesus and then he was driven to tell others. In the process of trying to inform and reform his own religious group, he ended up dying for the truth that he found on the pages of the Word. His death declared just how much he believed what he had discovered. While trying to tell the truth he had discovered to others, he was killed. In His death he did and said more than he could have done or said with his life.

Yes, Martin Luther, like many others when reading the truth in its purest form, found true life. He had to step away from the bondage of the wisdom of his day and go to the truth of God's Word to find truth, freedom, forgiveness, and true salvation.

Let me simply say here, we must look beyond what others say and study the Word for ourselves so that we too will become sure of our redemption in the blood sacrifice of Jesus, the Christ. But as you have now been made aware, there are weakened Bibles, translated from different and faulty manuscripts that can condemn those who are afraid to study the facts for themselves. I am simply trying to challenge you to search out these issues for yourself, and not simply take even our peers' word for it. The stakes are too high to simply turn our heads.
If we have a revival, it will be because God burdens us to look further than the denominational talking points to find the facts!

May the Lord Jesus Christ be with you as you search for TRUTH!

Power # 2 The Pulpit on Fire

There is no question that the future of America's third awakening rests in the pulpit. The men of God were before and still are the center spokes in the transporting of a dead society into an age of revival, awakening, repentance, purity and spiritual actions as well as power with God. How can America become on fire for God if the pulpits are soaked with confusion, compromise, ignorance, arrogance and stubborn pride. But the greatest enemy of the modern man of God is a love for the world and a desire to be accepted by their peers.

George Whitefield laid the blame of dead churches squarely on the backs of the clergy. He said, "I am persuaded the generality of preachers talk of an unknown and unfelt Christ. The reason why congregations have been so dead is because they had dead men preaching to them. How can dead men beget living children?[lviii]

I personally believe he is right. How can the laymen and women be on fire for God if the pulpit is not? The man of God cannot take the people into a repentant, spirit-filled relationship with God if he is not there himself. Therefore, the need for your pastor to read this book as well as your repentance and prayers for your pastor are of great necessity. History teaches us that in order for a Great Awakening to come, the preacher must be on fire, standing on the inerrant, unchanging Word.

Power # 3 The Power of Prayer

Any student of history knows that revival simply will not come without prayer. The revival scripture given to us by God is very specific. II

Chronicles 7:14, "if my people, which are called by my name, shall humble themselves, and pray, and seek my face, and turn from their wicked ways; then will I hear from heaven, and will forgive their sin, and will heal their land."

- *'my people—'*   *Awakening is for God's People*

- *'humble themselves—'*   *Attitude of heart and opposite of pride*

- *'pray—'*   *Communication, fellowship with God*

- *'seek my face—'*   *Desiring God's attention and approval*

- *'repentance—'*   *Turn from sin, from own way*

These are not hard to understand. God made an essential part of revival that is God-given-prayer. But notice the type of prayer—humble, repentant, desiring God's will. Also, revival is not dependent on the repentance of the lost but the repentance of the called of God. Therefore, the Word of God, the man of God, and the prayers of

God's people will invite or reject the Grate Awakening III.

Will it happen? I think that is still a question. Now, there is no question that you and I need a Great Awakening III! However, that history is yet to be written. It is being made even as I write this to you. Both you and I are the makers or breakers of the Great Awakening III. The one who will answer the question is you. It has happened before. It can happen again. God has always reserved himself a remnant. II Chronicles 7:14 tells us it is possible. That's the good news.

Let us learn from our own, as well as from biblical history. We must pray for, stand on, and look to an America full of deep love for the God of the Bible.

> *I charge thee therefore before God, and the Lord Jesus Christ, who shall judge the quick and the dead at his appearing and his kingdom; Preach the word; be instant in season, out of season; reprove, rebuke, exhort with all longsuffering and doctrine. For the time will come when they will not endure sound doctrine; but after their own lusts shall they heap to themselves teachers, having itching ears; And they shall turn away their ears from the truth, and shall be turned unto fables. But watch thou in all things, endure afflictions, do the*

work of an evangelist, make full proof
of thy ministry (2 Timothy 4:1-5).

This is our charge now. Will *you* be the Whitefield of 2021? Will *you* be the Moody of 2021?

The answer is...it's really up to you and me! We will see.

References:

[i] Laughlin "Excess Radiogenic Argon in Pegmatite Minerals," Journal of Geophysical Research, Vol. 74, 1969, p.6684.

[ii] Darwin, Charles, The Origin of Species, Vol. 2, 6th Ed., p.49.

[iii] Neville, George T., "Fossils in Evolutionary Perspective," Science Progress, Vol. 48, January 1960, pp.1,3.

[iv] Morris, Henry M., Scientific Creationism, Creation-Life Publishers, San Diego, California, 1976, p.277.

[v] Ibid 4.

[vi] Matthew's L.H., *The Origin of Species,* by Charles Darwin, J.M. Dent and Sons, Ltd., London, 1971, p. 10.

[vii] Federer, William, *America's God and Country Encyclopedia of Quotations* Fame Publishing, Inc. Coppell, Texas 1994, pp. 324, 325.

[viii] Ibid, 7, pp. 10, 11.

[ix] Ibid, 7, pp. 247, 248, 249.

[x] Ibid, 7, p. 144.

[xi] Ibid, 7, p. 145.

[xii] Ibid, 7, pp. 145, 146.

[xiii] Ibid, 7, p. 146.

[xiv] Ibid, 7, p. 153.

[xv] Ibid, 7, p. 322.

[xvi] Ibid, 7, p. 324.

[xvii] Ibid, 7, pp. 4, 5.

[xviii] Ibid, 7, p. 8.

[xix] Ibid, 7, pp. 8, 9.

[xx] Ibid, 7, pp. 9, 10.

[xxi] Ibid, 7, p. 14.

[xxii] Ibid, 7, pp. 634, 635, 636.

[xxiii] Ibid, 7, p. 637.

[xxiv] Ibid, 7, pp. 637, 638.

[xxv] Ibid, 7, p. 639.

[xxvi] Ibid, 7, pp. 637, 638.

[xxvii] Ibid, 7, pp.642, 643.

[xxviii] Ibid, 7, p. 107.

[xxix] Ibid, 7, p. 107.

[xxx] Ibid, 7, p. 108.

[xxxi] Ibid, 7, p. 317.

[xxxii] Ibid, 7, p. 318.

[xxxiii] Ibid, 7, p. 318.

[xxxiv] Ibid, 7, pp. 275, 276.

[xxxv] Bennett William J. *The Spirit of America, Our Sacred Honor,* Broadman and Holman Publishers, 1997, p. 219.

[xxxvi] Ibid, 35, p. 386.

[xxxvii] Ibid, 35, p. 41.

[xxxviii] Ibid, 35, pp.34, 35.

[xxxix] Catherine Millard, *The Rewriting of America's History,* Horizon House Publishers, 1991, p. 265.

[xl] Ibid, 37, pp. 313-314.

[xli] Ibid, 37, pp. 396, 397.

[xlii] Unger Merrill F., Th.D., Ph.D., *Unger's Bible Handbook, Moody Press, 1966 Chicago, IL*, pp. 882, 883.

[xliii] Ibid, 42, pp. 892-893.

[xliv] Pickering Wilbur, *The Identity of the New Testament Text,* (Nashville: Thomas Nelson Publishers, 1980), pp. 149, 150, 237.

[xlv] Burgon Dean John, *The Revision Revised,* Paradise, PA Conservative Classics, 54, xi, 270-277.

[xlvi] Hills Edward F., *The King James Defended*, Des Moines, IA: the Christian Research Press, 1973, p.219.

[xlvii] Colwell E.W., *What is the Best New Testament?,* Chicago: The University of Chicago Press, 1952, pp. 49, 53.

[xlviii] Fuller David Otis, *The Identity of the New Testament Text,* Grand Rapids, MI: Grand Rapids International Publications, 1984, p. 25.

[xlix] Westcott Arthur, *Life and Letters of Brooke Foss Westcott,* Vol 1, London: MacMillan and Co Limited, 1903, p. 47.

[l] Hort Arthur, *The Life and Letters of Fento John Anthony Hort,* Vol. 1 (New York: Macmillan and Co. 1986), p. 47.

[li] Ibid, 50, pp. 7, 41, 77.

[lii] Ibid, 50.

[liii] Ibid, 50 and 51, Vol. I, p. 400.

[liv] Ibid, 50, 51, 52, and 53, Vol. II, pp63, 92.

[lv] Morris Henry M., *A Creationist's Defense of the King James Bible,* (Institute for Creation Research, El Cajon, California, 1996), pp. 9-11.

[lvi] Jeffrey Grant R., *The Signature of God,* Frontier Research Publications, Inc. 1996, P.O. Box 129, Station "U" Toronto Ontario, M8Z5M4, pp. 14-15.

[lvii] Riplinger G.A., *The New Age Bible Versions,* 1993, Bible and Literature Missionary Foundation, 713 Cannon Blvd., Shelbyville, TN, 37160.

9 781952 465147